A
PSYCHOLOGY
FOR
PREACHING

HARPER'S MINISTERS PAPERBACK LIBRARY

A
PSYCHOLOGY
FOR
PREACHING

BY EDGAR N. JACKSON

PREFACE BY HARRY EMERSON FOSDICK

1817

HARPER & ROW, PUBLISHERS, SAN FRANCISCO
Cambridge, Hagerstown, New York, Philadelphia,
London, Mexico City, São Paulo, Sydney

First Harper & Row paperback edition published in 1981.

Library of Congress Cataloging in Publication Data

Jackson, Edgar Newman.
  A psychology for preaching.

  (Harper's ministers paperback library)
  1. Preaching. I. Title. II. Series.
BV4211.2.J3 1981   251   81-47430
ISBN 0-06-064111-8 (pbk.)   AACR2

81 82 83 84 85 10 9 8 7 6 5 4 3 2 1

CONTENTS

PASTORAL LANGUAGE AS BEHAVIOR:
A NEW INTRODUCTION

Pastors are people of the Word—the word read, written, and spoken. Anything relevant to the word is pertinent to preachers and to their function, personally and professionally.

More than at any time in history, people have in recent years studied the word in all its uses. It has been brought under scientific scrutiny by researchers from Abraham Maslow, who was concerned about what we say to ourselves, to Marshall McLuhan, who analyzed the impact of what is said to us. Language has been studied from Ernst Cassirer through Jurgen Ruesch to Theodore Thass-Rhienemann, and we cannot escape the impact of these assessments of words and their uses.

The skills of the demagogue are now being explored to see how they work and why, and the political implications of the word spoken from the pulpit are given a new significance as claims and counterclaims concerning their social power are exchanged. Probably not since Savonarola has the power of the spoken word from the pulpit been so carefully observed.

So the time is ripe for a careful and objective assessment of the current meaning of language as we hear it being used, especially from the pulpit. What is going on? Is it dangerous, or is it unimportant? What are the implications of long-held ideas about the relation of state and church? Has preaching moved out of the church into the television studio? Have irrational activity and the loss of institutional restraint beclouded the concept of preaching? And how has language research modified the function of the pulpit?

Traditionally, the special use of language that has characterized the pulpit has been centered around four functions. Sermons have usually sought to inspire, inform, facilitate personal growth, or manipulate people. In each of these four areas, recent studies have enhanced our understanding of the role of the preacher and the unusual form of communication that is the homily.

The concept of the nature of a human being is theological

in nature and is central to the process of preaching. It has been said that you can tell a preacher's concept of God by listening to a pastoral prayer. So also you can tell the concept of a human being by listening to the way a preacher preaches. The underlying assumptions come through loud and clear.

The goals assumed by a manipulator are quite different from the goals of a preacher who seeks to stimulate personal growth. Whenever we talk about inspiration, we must logically ask, "What would the nature of the inspired behavior be?" And we need to ask what kind of information is to be provided, and for what purpose.

Whether we admit it or not, the preaching process is geared to life as we experience it, both positively and negatively. Preaching can be a reaction to social anxiety that sends people scurrying back toward what appear to be older and safer ways of coping with life. So we have a crop of pulpiteers who are loudly proclaiming ideas that had more relevance a century ago than they do today. This escape from present reality is found at many levels of society, as Alvin Toffler showed in his book *Future Shock*. Instead of confronting changed circumstances and the need for wise adaptation, people often show a strong inclination to retreat from life and responsibility into glorified inanities and irrational attitudes.

Preaching changes as the needs of people change. A generation ago, I wrote a book on the therapeutic potential of preaching. *How to Preach to People's Needs* examined pressing problems reflected in the social and emotional behavior of congregations and made some suggestions for meeting those needs. Twenty-five years of rapid change lie between that day and this. What changes in the needs of people have emerged during these years, and how can the preaching process speak to these needs?

Perhaps we can best answer these questions by looking briefly at the changes that have been occurring in the social and emotional structure within which we live.

Science has made rapid strides in recent decades. Eighty percent of all the scientists who ever lived are alive and at work now—working with such sophisticated tools that a person can solve problems in one day that might have taken a lifetime before the age of computers. Cooperative ventures multiply the effectiveness of scientific programs, as we witnessed with the International Geophysical Year. Two responses have emerged. One group of preachers reject scientific theory, while they use scientific technology. They rely on an irrelevant authority to promote a cosmology and psychology that have long since been put to rest. But many other preachers seek to make the revelation of the New Testament valid for the emerging world of the future. Instead of retreating from the responsibility for the future, these preachers work to ease the pangs of birth for what is inevitable.

The impact of psychology has been felt in preaching. Psychology is the study of the meaning of behavior. Preaching is behavior, both on the part of those who preach and those who listen. A preacher can manipulate an audience skillfully when he or she takes advantage of the listener's neurotic guilt. Conversely, the preacher who values the sacred inner kingdom of people and wants to help nurture it can strengthen listeners and enhance their inner resources.

Psychological concern with the inner being has tended to

divert attention from the social process to the problems and possibilities of nurturing the core of being, where attitudes and motivations are paramount. In recent decades, however, the mass media have influenced the preaching process significantly. On one hand, manipulative preachers skillfully threaten listeners with dire consequences for failure to support programs financially. As a result, many programs that depend on uninstructed and unperceptive listeners grow in influence. At the same time, preachers who respect the inner beings of the audience and who encourage personal growth are forced from the airwaves by the cost and the competition of commercial enterprise. The television technology, which resists sober evaluation, is used without discrimination. And so more and more people are led to fear and dependence rather than to inner power and personal competence.

The growing interest in a multidisciplinary approach to health also influences preaching. Freud's emphasis on the therapeutic function of language has focused attention on the special utterance from the pulpit. Perceptive preachers cannot speak without being aware of how their words affect people. The powerful forms of communication that surround the word in worship, the varied art forms and supportive suggestions, amplify the meaning of the words themselves. Words can help and heal, or they can stimulate the emotions that harm and hurt. Our growing awareness of media technology's multi-faceted access to the human mind and emotion places an added responsibility on the privileged form of communication we call *preaching*.

Therefore, training programs in clinical pastoral education today have a special meaning. Preachers who are trained in the deeper psychological understanding of human response find that their pulpit utterances acquire a restraint that goes with growing responsibility. One cannot thunder and flash lightning from the pulpit without being aware of the consequences on the minds and emotions of the hearers. The more training a preacher has in the cause–effect processes that affect emotional responses, the more perception and restraint will mark the preacher's words. The more one knows about the subtle distinctions that exist in real, neurotic, and existential guilt, the more one realizes that blanket approaches to sin may well do more harm than good.

Wars, social unrest, and economic dislocation affect preaching both directly and indirectly. People are in constant interaction with the processes that surround and enmesh them. Homilies are both responses to and reactions against conditions that prevail in society. Sermons in recent years have been concerned about Vietnam, civil rights, and the social and economic stresses incident to the emergence of Third World nations. Here again, the preacher may present either a challenge to constructive change or a retreat from reality into illusions, delusions, or escapes that in the long run may compound the problems of life.

The struggle of depressed peoples and exploited nations seeking a unifying principle has led to the emergence of "liberation theology." All preaching makes implicit or explicit theological assumptions. When these assumptions challenge existing political, economic, and social orders, the lines of conflict are drawn. The conflict of church and state is illustrated by the killing of nuns at work among people whose humanity has been degraded, and by the killing of priests in their pulpits. The ethical assumptions of our society are moving into open conflict with repressive governments in matters of education, social reform, and the abuse of political power. The power and purpose of preaching acquire new status in the lives of people when they feel the church is fighting for human dignity and life itself.

When political power wants to restrain the influence of religion and reform, it first tries to frighten preachers into quiet conformity. This may be done by propagandizing the public. Deception and false issues can mislead the public and create suspicion of those who want to bring ethical issues into sharp focus. When military appropriations are expanding, for example, politicians try to frighten people into easy acceptance of greater expenditures by suggesting that enemy forces are encroaching. And when government makes loud, warlike sounds, the pulpit's message of peace and goodwill may be silenced or ignored.

Many social and political influences impinge on the role of the preacher in times of violence and rapid change. Preachers can advocate clear thinking and responsible action, or may capitulate to unbridled emotionalism, distorted reality, and a careless drift toward nuclear holocaust.

In addition to the many other forces that act on the role of the preacher in society, there is also the fact that language changes. The state of linguistic studies today makes it important for those who use language in the oral tradition of the past to examine assumptions, myths, fallacies, and methods. Preachers need to sharpen their basic tools of effective communication.

NEW INTRODUCTION

One significant change involves pitch and timbre of speech. The subtle emotional responses to differences between the speaking voice of men and women are now a major consideration in the pulpit. In some seminaries, half the graduates are women preparing for parish ministries. Some traditions are irrational about female voices in the pulpit. The changes that are coming about are rooted in a developing concept of personality. People are people first and possessors of sexual characteristics second. The women who enter the pulpit share a common education, an equal commitment, and a special endowment that can add immeasurably to the preaching profession's expression of spirituality, the quality of insight, and the understanding of inspiration. It would be a strange perversion of human values to discriminate against someone's vocal chords and pitch. Yet ancient and unreasoned prejudices are keeping women from having their rightful chance to proclaim the gospel.

Yet these "new" associations of voice and language bring a needed quality of nurturance into the pulpit. The inner discipline that emerges from clearer understanding of shared roles in life can enrich the ministry and give preaching a quality that may be less manipulative at the same time that it enriches perception and stimulates the growing edge of true spirituality.

New language studies also make it necessary to look at the scriptures more thoughtfully. The meaning of language is rooted in personal behavior. Language is personal behavior and thus is highly individualistic. No two people interpret the same words in the same way, because word meanings develop from experience. To demand inerrancy, absolute accuracy, is unresponsive to the unique and personal dimension of language. To preach the Word without trying to understand the personal meaning of any word is insensitive. To assume that anyone has the pure perception of scriptural truth falls far short of "rightly dividing the Word." In our day, with our understanding of the meaning of language as behavior, we must become increasingly sensitive to the inner climate of those who listen. And at the same time those who speak must accept the responsibility of understanding the inner kingdom we want to nurture.

Language studies not only throw new light on the scriptures but also compel preachers to realize that we are using an art form that depends on the inventive and creative skill of the artist as a communicator. Any art form is a special language. It calls for a special blending of disciplines, mastery of the medium, and dedication to the human fulfillment through the refinement of the art form. Even those who approach language in a reductionist manner cannot avoid recognizing the distinctions between the sensitive and the senseless.

In 1936, Alfred Jules Ayer published *Language, Truth and Logic*, a little book destined to have great influence on language theory both by what it said and the responses it generated. In it, Ayer carried to its conclusion the concept of logical positivism, which reduced language to its most simplistic form as a mechanical response to complex stimuli. Ayer said, "We shall maintain that no statement which refers to a 'reality' transcending the limits of all possible sense-experience can possibly have any literal significance; from which it must follow that the labors of those who have strived to describe such a reality have all been devoted to the production of nonsense."[1]

Ayer thus tried to obliterate preaching or any other metaphysical dimension of thought by making the significance of language minimal. Under such a stricture, no one could talk of God. Instead of being a vehicle of thought and feeling, language would be merely reflexive, adding nothing to the stimulus that provoked it. Furthermore, he said, "Our charge against the metaphysician is not that he attempts to employ the understanding in a field where it cannot possibly venture, but that he produces sentences which fail to conform to the conditions under which alone a sentence can be literally significant. Nor are we obliged to talk nonsense in order to show that all sentences of a certain type are necessarily devoid of literal significance."[2]

This reductionist approach to language could cut humankind off at its roots and deny its right to lofty aspirations. Ayer defined the significant sentence as one that can be verified in factual terms with scientifically accepted datum. This says that all traditionally philosophical inquiry is both irrelevant and invalid. Not only that, but he quite arbitrarily dispensed with the meaning of tradition and history, because no one can experience past events. So the long view of history and its meaning for culture would be abolished. He said, "For it must surely be admitted that, however strong the evidence in favor of historical statements may be, their truth can never become more than highly probable."[3]

Although Ayer sought to limit the function of language to the factual and verifiable, and thus to remove metaphysical thought and language from common usage, he did make some place for the art form: "The difference between the man who uses language scientifically and the man who uses it emotively is not that one produces sentences that are incapable of arousing emotion, and the other sentences which have no sense, but that the one is primarily concerned with the expression of true propositions, the other the creation of a work of art."[4]

So, although most sources of insight that would be the substance of religious communication were to be considered to be both irrelevant and nonsensical, special communications might remain valid primarily as art forms. The reductionist direction of Ayer's thought was rooted in a preoccupation with techniques and feared to admit that life itself can have meaning and can be meaningfully experienced by an individual. But if this assumption of meaning is made, then it is quite reasonable to be able to speak meaningfully about the experience.

For the religious communicator, the implications of Ayer's theories can be devastating, because, apart from some artful efforts, the substance and meaning of pastoral communication is "nonsense." According to reductionists, preaching is an exercise in futility, with no acceptable basis in reasoned thought. Similarly, the use of symbolic forms and traditional expressions in worship is irrelevant and invalid from the viewpoint of the scientific ideas that underlie our assumptions about life. Perhaps more than we realize, these ideas of Ayer have made many people feel that preaching is a futile activity and that listening to homilies is a waste of time and effort. If the theories of Ayer and others like him remain unchallenged, preachers might as well stop preaching, and the church might as well close up shop.

But important challenges to Ayer's basic premises have come from several sources. Because of space limitations, I can examine only a few of these sources here. I will explore these ideas under four different headings: (1) the physiology of speech, (2) the anthropology of speech, (3) the psychology of speech, and, finally, (4) the spiritual assumptions implicit in all speech. In doing this, I necessarily violate Ayer's concepts of language, but I will not fall into the trap of his reductionism by violating the nature of a human being.

A. T. W. Simeons, a British psychiatrist and student of the anatomy of the brain and human nervous system, wrote a book called *Man's Presumptuous Brain*. It is a study of behavior as a response to diencephalic impulses. The diencephalon is the most primitive portion of the brain; its prerational impact on behavior does not deal with issues of fact versus fiction but rather with needs for self-preservation. The emergence and basic use of speech was undoubtedly bound up with our early (and late) security system of group life. This connection places language in the mythic realm that Carl Jung speaks of, as a form of behavior well beyond the reach of reductionist theory.

Eilhard Von Domares, professor of anthropology and psychiatry at Yale University, claimed that the modification of life patterns among anthropoids produced a group of strong social ties, and from these intensified relationships emerged the rudiments of language. It appears, then, that early speech was a product of affective relationships, of the caring capacity, and that its development can never be effectively separated from its roots. Biological, physiological, and anthropological conditions have all made their contributions to speech, and no contemporary exploration of linguistics can ignore the meaning of these sources.

It is difficult to separate biological adaptation from primitive developments of speech, as studied by anthropologists. Carlton Laird says, "Babies and language are the essential ingredients of civilization, and speakers of language no more know where they come from than babies where they came from. . . . We know that we are inventing it every day of our lives . . . that language was due to some inner impulse, from something like 'a mature embryo pressing to be born.'"[5] Chomsky and Katz argue that a native language cannot be acquired, given its level of complexity and abstraction, unless children have innate knowledge of certain universal linguistic principles.[6]

If we can understand language only as we understand human beings, then we have moved into the realm of theology and the understanding of the human. This understanding introduces us to the spiritual dimension of being—a unique human endowment. Laird puts it thus: "If language is intimately related to being human, then when we study language, we are to a remarkable degree studying human nature. Similarly, we may expect language to be what it is because human beings are what they are. But we should not expect to study language by making inferences from other fields of study."[7] In other words, to apply mathematical logic to human communication, as Ayer has done, is irrelevant: the human purpose of language cannot be reasonably deduced from other forms of analysis.

So we come full circle in our examination of the relevance

of religious language and concepts to human speech. People who look at language in its more human aspects not only express the totality of the human experience, subjective and objective, but also recognize the variants that determine whether or not expression is artfully and creatively done. To this extent, then, pastoral communication has validity and significance.

Psychological study adds immeasurably to our understanding of the validity of pastoral language. In truth, the Word becomes flesh and is a living presence among us. By listening intently to human speech: to its quality, content, abnormalities, and timbre; to what is said and what is not said—in such ways we gain an insight into the psyche or soul that may be as revealing as a dream. In fact, the significance of free association is built on the significance of the obliquely revealed inner processes of mind and emotion. True communication may be achieved only as deep speaks to deep and as the total person is in resonance. As Pierre Tielhard de Chardin might say, the door that opens to the Noosphere is responsive to the energy of the Spirit that is disciplined through words.

Healthy speech, then is the behavior of a healthy individual, and disturbed speech is the symptom of disturbance. This may explain why, in the treatment of forms of speech disfunction, psychoanalytic intervention does not usually prove to be effective: the conscious mind must be involved in the processes that change the expression of conscious mental activity. The language of the pastor approaches the person therapeutically via the conscious mind. But it is equally true that speech, personally and humanly, is deeply rooted in other dimensions of consciousness and involves the total being in the complicated behavior we call *language*. So the pastor uses consciousness to bring other forms of mental activity into a therapeutic context. In contrast, the psycho-analyst usually approaches the lower levels of consciousness in order to modify conscious perception and conscious forms of behavior.

From the psychological point of view, language is not merely a matter of speech, as important as that may be. Psychosomatic research gives us many illustrations of body language, where the behavior of the organism takes a more direct form for expressing its emotional state. The assumption of psychosomatic treatment is that illness is meaningful organic behavior. The symptom is the effect, and the treatment can be most effectively directed when the cause is clearly discerned. This research verifies the importance of the subjective use of language to modify the internal state of an individual. If body chemistry is tied to emotional states, then the use of speech that touches the inner recesses of emotion and meaning for life clearly has a special validity. So the pastor's role in therapeutic communication is not only verified psychologically, but is also given a status of the first order in helping to develop an inner being that is adequate to cope with life.

Art forms are characterized by highly individualized modes of expression, so the artful presentation of ideas through preaching is strongly tinged by the preacher's personal qualities. It could safely be said that all preaching is autobiographical, because both the subject matter and its treatment emerge from the depths of personal being. This aspect makes preaching both a challenge and a hazard.

The challenge comes from the personal authenticity of sincerity and conviction. But it is well to remember that sincerity is a secondary virtue. One can be sincerely mistaken, and so sincerely misleading. Thus a listener is doubly vulnerable to preachers who proclaim with powerful emotion what they cannot sustain with sound judgment or careful exploration of the facts. The line between careless preaching and demagoguery is hard to discern. But sound religion can be abused by sociopaths whose need for power over others obscures the obligation for wise restraint in the privileged utterance of the pulpit.

Preachers engaging in exhortation, interpretation, and inspiration may be tempted to use what is sometimes spoken of as "homiletic license." But this license can distort reality. Reality in and of itself may be a rather static thing. To make reality more interesting, one may feel a strong impulse to improve on it. The inventive and creative skill of the artist can make reality more interesting without distorting its essence.

The preacher who finds life worth living can help renew life for others. The challenge is to create the vision that can be seen clearly and be responded to with enthusiasm. Communication can vividly outline the role of religion, not to create new facts but to supply richer meaning to the facts of life that already exist. The insights of psychology and physics can bring new life to the revelation of the New Testament, which is more pertinent now than ever before in history.

NEW INTRODUCTION

There was a time when the main preoccupation of religion was the saving of individuals from their own self-destructive behavior. Now for the first time in history, the main preoccupation is the saving of the only God-conscious creatures who ever lived from the self-destruction of all humanity—and much of the rest of God's creation.

Our day needs preaching. The conditions demand it, and the possibilities for using language creatively are there waiting for us to rise to the opportunity. Preachers with clear voices, who can speak to the present without neglecting our responsibility for the future, must be heard.

In the pages that follow, we address ourselves to developing a perspective on the role of the preacher speaking to a rapidly changing and deeply threatened humanity. The initial research recorded in these pages has aroused interest, leading to many further monographs and theses. Many more are needed. I hope this restatement of concerns will lead to new and even more pertinent exploration in the days ahead.

E. N. J.
Corinth, Vermont
August 1981

A
PSYCHOLOGY
FOR
PREACHING

INTRODUCTION TO THE FIRST EDITION

*T*HE RAPID GROWTH of interest in pastoral counseling and the resources for pastoral care have brought
into focus a problem that has been of concern to many
pastors. Traditional preaching has been authoritative, in
the non-personal framework of worship, and bound about

by certain long-standing traditions that prescribe its form and function. The new methods of pastoral counseling bring into the counseling room a new discipline that is not authoritative, is most personal, and is as yet free from the restraints that ecclesiastical tradition might place upon it.

It would seem that these two important functions of the modern pastor are contradictory and antithetical. However, it is our feeling that this is not essentially so. The disciplines may be different in kind but not in purpose. Modern insight into personality and human relations may give a new and helpful direction to the oldest form of group therapy, that of worshipping together. It is our hope that we may here be able to throw an experimental bridge across the gap between preaching and counseling.

How can preaching be made to serve as an aid in the counseling function? How can the counseling function as employed by the pastor make use of those spiritual values that are traditional to enrich his ministry to individuals?

It would be well to keep in mind that the following pages are not a comprehensive study of the function of preaching. There is a demand on the pulpit for education, information, inspiration, exhortation and exposition. The content of some sermons must serve a different purpose from the content of others. The area of preaching that can pave the way for counseling must be limited by the variety of demands on the pulpit. But the attitude of the pulpit need have no limitations as it makes people important, faith positive, and the ministry accessible.

New insights growing from a careful study of what takes place in groups throw light upon the preaching function so that it may become an instrument for serving the needs of persons in groups at the same time that it prepares the way for meeting the special needs of those who seek counsel.

While I am solely responsible for shortcomings in this study, I am indebted for any adequacy it may have to the late Dr. Halford E. Luccock, for encouragement and advice; to Dr. Wellman J. Warner, president of the World Congress on Group Psychotherapy, for aid with technical aspects of the study; and to thousands of persons who through nine years of clinical experience and twenty-seven years of preaching have been alive to me as I have been alive to them.

EDGAR N. JACKSON

Mamaroneck, N.Y.
February, 1961

1

ENGAGING THE MIND

*I*T IS probably well for the preacher to face up to the fact
that he has inherited one of the most difficult vehicles
for effecting human experience. That so many people have
been so deeply affected by preaching is a tribute to the forcefulness of the witness of the inspired person.

On the other hand, the necessity of trying to be inspiring on a week to week basis calls for all of the ingenuity that a preacher can develop. It is at this point that recent insights into human responsiveness that have been made by psychologists are particularly helpful.

This first chapter seeks to show how psychological insights can be applied to the technical phase of pulpit communication, and the subsequent chapters indicate how these insights can be applied to more basic principles of preaching method and sermon content.

Edgar Dale, in *Audio-Visual Methods of Teaching*,[1] presents a cone of experience which indicates the relative effectiveness of different mediums of instruction. Direct, purposeful experience is most effective, for it involves most of the person. Contrived experiences come next, and then follow dramatic participation, demonstrations, field trips, exhibits, motion pictures, still pictures with recordings, visual symbols, and last of all, the medium the preacher uses, that of verbal symbols.

We know that effective preaching has always been able to use verbal symbols to create pictures, to demonstrate life experience, and to stimulate the type of direct, purposive action that ultimately becomes the most effective form of learning. What we need is the insight of the modern student into human responses, and that effective communication which can help us to sharpen our traditional tool of human speech so that it is more direct, more vigorous and more effective.

When Francis Asbury preached in this country, he found that his message was not welcomed at first. He

18

records that in Westchester "the people were insensible to my preaching." Also he says, "They would not listen, for they were interested in many other things." It was not until he had become acclimated to the New World that he was able to catch the people's interest. When he became a part of them, understood their interests and needs, he was able to communicate with them and stir a real response.

Attention can be sustained for long periods of time only when the hearer feels a direct relationship with the speaker. The sense of communication must be continually renewed or revitalized. Long-distance cable communication is made possible by boosters every few miles to increase the signal. What is true of distance in an electrical impulse is also true of the intensity of a direct communication. It must have a booster every few minutes to keep it vital and alive.

Two psychologists watched a number of students in a library. With stopwatches in hand they measured student attention spans, and concluded that they kept their minds on their work only 60% of the time. "The rest of the time is spent drawing doodles, watching others, gazing blankly into space . . ." What is true of mental activity in study seems also to be true when direct communication is involved. "It has been estimated that a class listening to a teacher, an employee listening to his boss, or an audience listening to a lecture has serious lapses of attention every seven minutes. The expert public speaker jerks attention back by telling a story, making a demonstration, or doing something unusual about every five minutes. Interest, action or noise will renew attention."

The fact that a minister has a certain status and prestige does not free him from the responsibility to present his message as winsomely and as well as possible. Too often a man who has won the hearts of his people as a pastor seems to feel that he has earned the right to be a careless craftsman in the pulpit.

No one ever earns the right to be uninteresting in the pulpit. Those who think so are exacting tribute from their total ministry, and should be aware of it. A fundamental principle of good education is that people accept more readily whatever has been actively related to their field of interest.

A student may fail in mathematics until he needs it in an engineering course. Then this new need brings dead arithmetic to life.

Jesus had the great gift of making his words relate directly to his hearers. Since metaphors were an intrinsic part of Jewish speech, and feelings were inherent in the daily living of an emotional people, his listeners were keenly responsive to his way of speaking.

A minister can most effectively reach his congregation through a constant awareness of their interests. If he comes down from his ivory tower only once a week, his people will see him—but will they hear him? As a teen-ager said of her pastor, "When he preaches it is like dropping a custard pie. It splatters over everything, but doesn't hit anything very hard."

A healthful variation on the ivory tower approach is for the preacher who dwells intimately with his people through the week to rise up from among them on Sunday to give a new and holier perspective to their common needs and interests.

A successful salesman wants to sell his product. He is interested in the customer because he must relate the potential buyer to the product. He studies his approach, because he knows how important it is to get his "toe in the door." The preacher who is successful is always seeking a conviction. He cannot get it unless he can first of all get his "intellectual toe" into the door of the mind of his listener. The opening sentences of a sermon can best serve their purpose if the preacher deliberately and skillfully makes the hearer feel that he is involved.

How we have sinned at this point! Think of the sermons you have preached. I can think of some I have inflicted on innocent and long suffering people. How many times have you tried to impress people with your knowledge of New Testament Greek by starting out with an erudite exposition of a text? How often have you waited a moment to make sure that everyone was comfortable, only to put them into intellectual slumber by an excursion into Biblical history? Or again, how often have you opened with a quotation from a church historian, a Post-Nicean Father, or a patron saint of your denomination? What better warning could you give your hearers that the next half hour is to be spent centuries away in time and thousands of miles away in space? In effect you are like the salesman who says, "I know you don't want any of this, but here's my line anyway," or like the preacher whom one woman describes as "always scratching us where we don't itch."

Often people want what the preacher has to give but

do not realize it because his message is presented in words and phrases that are unfamiliar, or in a manner that is too general for specific application. In every congregation there are people who are battling a bad conscience, or are frustrated by home situations that are unhappy, or have jobs they want to escape. They are in need of the guidance, perspective and new attitude that their minister can give. Yet too often the preacher starts where he is and moves about only in ideas which seem important to him, and the needy listener fails to find a relationship to his own need.

The preacher's task is certainly complicated by the fact that he is dealing with many persons at the same time and must be general enough to protect the sensibilities of individuals. A surgeon operates on one person at a time. A salesman usually sells to one person at a time. A psychiatrist talks with one person at a time. But the preacher must use a mass approach to his people. No wonder some pastors indulge in sermons that have the impact of a custard pie. But, having said that, we must narrow the task of the preacher and define more sharply the area within which he must work. Although he is inevitably dealing with a group, yet he knows people well enough to be aware of universal needs, and he should know his own people intimately enough to shape and direct his message so that it will be most helpful.

Also the preacher suffers from an educational problem that is not of his own creating. Though he is expected to minister to people, his ministerial training is usually completely or largely lacking in the courses that would make it possible for him to develop both practical and theoretical understanding of people. Courses in practical theology or pastoral care are orphans at many seminaries. Courses in preaching are carried on *in vacuo* because the student is always dealing with an imaginary congregation. Then, too, the average seminary student is emerging from his own adolescence. He is apt to be so preoccupied with the forming of his own philosophy of life that he has little time or thought for the needs of others.

The preaching habits of the early years of his ministry may persist through maturity if they are not carefully and frequently reexamined. If the early preaching practice is self-centered, or idea-centered rather than person-centered, the preacher may never develop his capacity for relating to his people. This seems to be borne out by the findings of Dr. Reuel L. Howe in his retraining program for ministers. "As a result of innumerable conversations with these men," he says, "certain aspects of the problem become clearer. One comment occurs again and again, namely, that they were not really prepared for work with people. One man put it this way, 'I received the best theological education available; but it was education for theological study and teaching, and not training for the work of the ministry.' Man after man has said that what he knew about the Bible, Church History, Theology and other departments of theological learning had no relevance for the flood of human problems that overwhelmed him from the beginning of his ministry. Time after time men said that the real training for the work they had to do was on the job and by trial and error. Repeatedly they referred to themselves as the 'blind leading the blind.' "

Dr. Howe found that the majority of students were

critical of their training "in that there was an overemphasis on subject matter and underemphasis on people, their relationships and their needs." Probably most ministers fall into one of three groups. Some have a natural warmth and feeling for people, and that quality will dominate their ministry whether they are trained for it or not. Others have personality defects that make it easier for them to reject people than to accept them. No simple study of techniques of relationship will help them for they need basic psychological and social healing themselves.

A large and important group are those normal, healthy individuals who are anxious to improve their techniques for relating themselves and their message to their people. They are the ones who will gladly accept the insights of those social sciences that have been studying group procedures and psychological approaches. The average minister is not so much interested in criticizing his training, or excusing his shortcomings, as he is in sharpening his practical and intellectual tools so that he may work more effectively in the present he has and the future he expects.

Those who make a careful study of approaches to people for advertising purposes recognize the importance of freshness of approach. Certainly those who would present something as valuable as the Gospel should not wrap it up in stale speech. It is no compliment to a congregation to serve them a warmed-over sermon. Great truths can be presented again and again in different ways, but what happens when you say, "A few years ago in a former parish" or "Some of you may have heard this before, but," or "Pardon me if I repeat"? Many good things may go into the barrel, but few good things come out of it. How fortunate it is that the barrel is becoming a less important part of the furnishing for a minister's study. Every congregation is different, and deserves the compliment of a completely new and fresh presentation of sermonic material.

Any pot of message will come to a boil more quickly if a fire of self-related interest is kindled under it. Part of the success of Russell H. Conwell's "Acres of Diamonds" was found at this point. Though he preached that sermon a thousand times, he never preached it the same way twice. He would try to find out all he could about the possibilities of the town and the people to whom he was to preach, and then would relate to them directly the story of the man who sold his property to go in search of diamonds only to find that his old farm had within it the largest diamond deposit in the world. He never failed to stir people because he had an important message and because he obviously thought his hearers important enough to have the message tailored to fit their particular situation.

If it is important to relate to your hearers, it is desirable also to relate to them as quickly as possible. Harry Emerson Fosdick was a master at the art of quickly identifying with his congregation. I re-read a half-dozen of his sermons, and these were the opening sentences I found.

"Amid the uncertainties of modern psychology, one thing seems assured: more people suffer from a humiliating sense of inferiority than ever has been supposed."

"Our morning's thought concerns one of the most significant aspects of human life: our representative capacity."

"Our thought starts this morning with the plain fact

that it is not always easy to tell the difference between right and wrong."

"We are concerned today about a factual personal problem so nearly universal in its application that we need not be bothered by its exceptions."

"Our morning subject, Handicapped Lives, probably takes us all in."

"There is a picture that haunts the imagination these days concerning which I wish to speak seriously with you . . ."

There is never any doubt as to whom he speaks. It is you. Again and again, in one opening sentence he relates the subject of the sermon to the interest of the listener. No wonder hundreds of thousands listened intently to his preaching for forty years. They knew he talked to them. They knew he felt they were important enough to take them into consideration at the very beginning. Such relatedness is not flattery; it is common courtesy.

Harold Roupp, who was unusually successful in dealing with college students, often started his sermon by presenting a proposition. He had been an effective debater in college, and developed a technique that immediately created interest. He said, in effect, "I am not going to give you a one-sided picture. I am going to wrestle with this proposition in full view of all of you." Then he would go ahead to present the negative side with full honesty and candor, and then come surging back with a positive argument that carried his listeners with him to his conclusion. There was a certain amount of intellectual daring in the process that appealed to college students who were debating propositions in their own minds. They felt honored to have a chance to go behind the scenes of life with a mature mind, and labor together over a problem. They did not want one-sided inspiration or exhortation. They wanted an experience of honest intellectual combat and growth. They got it.

Some may object that such a procedure is risky; that it is risky to give more than one side to a congregation. Consider, if you will, the greater risk of creating a lopsided faith that is equipped to handle only straw men. If our people cannot be trusted to enter into the struggle for truth in partnership with their minister, their faith is too feeble a thing to save the world.

In experiments related to its indoctrination program, the Army tried various approaches to its men. To one group they presented a one-sided picture with an exhortation. To another they gave both sides of the argument with a reasoned statement for their conclusion. They found that:

1. Presenting the arguments on both sides of an issue was more effective than giving only the arguments supporting the point being made, in the case of individuals who were initially opposed to the point of view being presented.

2. For men who were already convinced of the point of view being presented, however, the inclusion of arguments on both sides was less effective for the group as a whole than presenting only the arguments favoring the general position being advocated.

3. Better educated men (high school graduates) were more favorably affected by presentation of both sides;

27

poorly educated men were more affected by the communication which used only supporting arguments. 4. The group for which the presentation giving both sides was least effective was the group of poorly educated men who were already convinced of the point of view being advocated. 5. An important incidental finding was that omission of a relevant argument was more noticeable and detracted more from effectiveness in the presentation using arguments on both sides than in the presentation in which only one side was discussed.

These conclusions of the Army's experiment offer no simple rule of thumb. For intelligent people it seems important that an intellectually fair presentation of any problem is essential to a good hearing. For the moderately well educated an honest presentation of differences of view adds drama and interest to the discussion. For the poorly educated such a method may add confusion. Again, we are obliged to tailor our message to fit our people, not only at the point of interest, but also at the point of their ability to respond.

I once served a church in a small New England manufacturing town. My sermons at first seemed to go over like balloons. I talked the matter over with a district superintendent who had had experience in such a church. He wisely said, "Most of your people work at machines. Their attention span is short and related to routine actions. If it were not so, they might lose their fingers. On Sunday they think the same way. Try short illustrations and quick points." I did, and the response was excellent. The sermons would have rated poorly in a class on homiletics, but they reached my people at their level of mental activity.

While effective preaching must engage both the mind and the feelings, it seems that the mind must be reached first. Both Doctors Roupp and Fosdick found it helpful to state a problem in as simple and personal terms as possible so that the listener would feel it was his problem, and then, with the preacher, enter into the task of seeking a solution.

Dr. Harold Cooke Phillips has been successful in holding people's interest for long periods of time. He uses few illustrations but brings to his preaching an earnestness and intensity that is commanding. But he does not depend on these personal qualities alone. He is intent for a purpose and that purpose is to come to grips with real problems for real people. I turned at random in a book of his sermons and found these opening sentences:

"It is a fair question which we put to ourselves in our times—'What is the reward of Christian living?'"

"We shall speak today of the wisdom of Jesus as it bears on what is considered the greatest social problem of our age—the problem of war."

With such opening sentences the minds of the hearers are engaged. He does not imply that the congregation already knows all he is going to say. He does not imply that what he is going to say is unimportant for them. He makes the sermon a common mental exercise in which they are invited to share.

This seems to have been the method that Jesus used. We have only fragments of his sermons, but we note that again and again there was an immediate and strong response to what he said. The listeners had been mentally engaged. They questioned him. They questioned themselves. They reacted. "They rose up, and thrust him out of the city." Any way we look at it, we must admit there are very few modern preachers who stimulate so vigorous a response. We may be sure Jesus spent little time sawing sawdust. He ripped into the real problems of people and his age. He generated real participation and response.

If we are to engage the active interest and participation of our congregations, it is good strategy to open a sermon with a question, a problem, or a difficulty.

Contrary to generally accepted practice, it is psychologically sound to make your strongest point first. Aristotle notwithstanding, it has been found that starting with a weak point and building to a climax is unsound and ineffective. Harold Sponberg prepared two phonograph records of the same material, but changed the order of presenting the material. To one group of students he presented the speech in a traditional form. To the other group of students he presented the speech in a revised form, with the strongest point first and the others following in order of their strength. He examined both classes on three points. What had they remembered? How had their minds been changed? After a lapse of time, he asked further questions that checked their memories. At all three points he found that his students remembered better, remembered longer and were affected more by the talk that presented the strong point first.

The logic of this seems quite simple. If the first material is weak, we lose our hearers at the beginning, and even strong material cannot win back their attention as effectively as catching it with potent material at the beginning and holding it with the best we have as long as it is effective. If the opening material is strong, the hearers will help to furnish their own climax. If it is weak, they won't even be there at the end, mentally.

Getting the attention of a congregation is like wooing a girl. You must keep working at it. You can't get her attention and then forget all about her. Even presenting the strongest point first doesn't solve the problem of keeping attention through the rest of the sermon. Since our thoughts tend to wander, it's good strategy for a preacher to use a graphic illustration, a bit of humor, or a series of questions every few minutes to "jerk back the attention" of his listeners.

Humor is useful in getting attention and holding it, but humor is a two-edged sword. One must use it with care or it will do more cutting than is intended. Within the context of a sermon, this is particularly true. The humor that is accepted at an after-dinner speech is not acceptable in a sermon. In fact, humor that is only humor has no place in a sermon. The story that is inserted merely to make people laugh cheapens the sermon.

But there are elements of humor that are both useful and fitting. Perhaps there is no task more difficult for a preacher than that of preaching the annual sermon on raising the budget. If there is ever a time when a light touch is needed to stimulate a heavy touch, it is at such a time. In opening just such a sermon, Dr. Fosdick invoked the light touch with a bit of humor that was neither irrelevant nor cheapening. He said, "There was once a preacher who intended to beg his congregation to listen to the Gospel's cheerful tidings, but his tongue slipped and, falling into a Spoonerism, he asked them instead to listen to the Gospel's tearful chidings. Many a minister in these difficult days, endeavoring to raise the church's budget, will thus fall from cheerful tidings into tearful chidings."

Another pastor dealt with the matter of instituting a unified budget and financial program for his church by indicating that it was their effort to "put all their begs in one ask it." He illustrated his point by telling of a wealthy woman who had visited a nearby silver fox farm to pick out some pelts for her coat. After examining some of the animals for a while she asked the owner in a haughty tone, "How often do you skin them?" After a short pause he answered, "Only once, Madam. It makes them nervous." Then he quickly added that repeated appeals for money make church members nervous, and that it would be their effort to let the one united appeal meet all of the financial needs of the church so that their important efforts could be directed to more spiritually productive activity.

Abuse of humor can be a serious industrial hazard for the minister, but the element of surprise that is important in good humor can be used all through a sermon, and with good effect. Often it may be simply a phrase that is needed. Dr. Halford E. Luccock was a master at the art of the cleverly turned phrase. He lightened up a chapel talk by referring to the Henry Ford Museum as "Henry Ford's graveyard of American antiquities." No one rolled in the aisle with side-splitting laughter, but there was many a pleasant smile and appreciative glance. He also used mild satire with telling effect. His "St. John's by the Gas Station" has become one of America's famous churches. Also he used the Biblical quotation in a surprising context; without making the scripture trivial, he did make it have new meaning by giving it a fresh relationship.

Also, Dr. Luccock can teach us much about using the apt quotation or verse of poetry to drive home a point with the light touch. Speaking of those pulpit patrons of the irrelevant who operate in a "fog of gentility," he quoted,

I wish that my room had a floor,
I don't so much care for a door,
But this walking around without touching the ground
Is getting to be quite a bore.

Such a quatrain does quickly and deftly what ought to be done. It gives a picture, and it has both an element of surprise and a bit of humor.

Or in speaking of the rich fool of the parable, Luccock quoted Walter Rauschenbusch, who said, "This man was a sublimated chipmunk, gloating over a bushel of pignuts." It is humorous to make such an analogy, but it is also a telling point that the picture gives. Or the wise use of a proverb like, "There are no pockets in a shroud" may say more than pages of full exposition.

How quickly he relates the idea of the parable of the ten virgins to the complacent pew-sitter by this bit of doggerel:

In the world's broad field of battle,
In the bivouac of life,

> You will find the average layman
> Represented by his wife.

Yes, you smile but you get the point. Similarly there is an element of surprise, with a hard-driven point, in even such a couplet as this:

> Organized charity, scrimped and iced
> In the name of a cautious, statistical Christ.

Dr. Charles W. Gilkey employed surprise with effect in paraphrasing the story of the Good Samaritan for a college audience.

"A certain Freshman went from home to college and she fell among critics who said that she had no style, that her manners were awkward and that she had an unattractive personality. Then they stripped her of her self-confidence, her enthusiasm, and her courage, and departed, leaving her hurt and lonely and half dead.

"And when the seniors saw it they were amused, saying, 'What a good job the sophomores are doing on that freshman,' and they passed on the other side.

"In like manner, the juniors also, when they saw it, smiled and said, 'Yea, verily, for she hath not the makings of a good sorority girl.' And they passed by on the other side.

"But a certain special student, as she went about, came where the freshman was, and when she saw the freshman she was moved with compassion, and came to her and bound up her wounds, pouring on sympathy and understanding. And she took the freshman to her room and set her on her feet again, and brought her unto her own circle and was a friend to her.

"Which of these, thinkest thou, proved neighbor to her that fell among the critics? Go thou and do likewise."

The use of the old form of speech and the familiar narrative in a new setting creates and keeps interest. It is fit and proper for sermon use.

While pulpit utterance requires a certain type of dignity, it does not need to be dead. Mr. Spurgeon once pointed out the difference between the Devil and a Deacon with these words, "The Scripture says, 'resist the Devil, and he will flee from you,' but 'resist the deacons and they will fly at you.'"

Nor is all humor intentional. The naive may say surprising things; witness the preacher who combined eloquence with a forgetfulness of the interests of young men at a YMCA Sunday evening service. After treading lightly over the story of the ten virgins, he came to a climax after this fashion, saying, "And now, my young men, where would you rather be—in the light with the five wise virgins or in the dark with the five foolish ones." The result was almost as electric as when the aged pastor preached feelingly on Balaam and his perspicacious donkey, only to end his post-sermon prayer with this exhortation, "and, oh God, get those faltering people off of their asses." No benediction was needed.

A light touch can help to bring perspective into a situation. Dr. William Temple, the dignified Archbishop of Canterbury, dealt with Dr. Reinhold Niebuhr's preoccupation with sin in these words:

> At Swanwick, when Niebuhr had quit it,
> Said a young man: "At last I have hit it,
> Since I cannot do right
> I must find out tonight
> The best sin to commit—and commit it."

In pulpit speech there is no need to use a lecture to do what a limerick can do better.

Perhaps Dean Charles R. Brown of Yale can sum up that matter for us. He knew humor and employed it with wisdom. "It is not well for a minister to go out of his way six inches to make a joke. But when some unexpected turn comes to him naturally in the treatment of a great truth, he is unwise to turn aside in order to avoid it. Let him study the great masters of delicate humor in the literature of the race. Let him use, if he will, those lighter statements which bring a sense of surprise. Let him employ 'the finest of the wheat' in this matter of humor, just in passing, with a touch and go, never waiting for a laugh, and he will find that by this method he has added greatly to his power of spiritual appeal."

This leads quite naturally to the discipline of preparation. One is not apt to find the light touch or the sense of relatedness-to-his-people if he does not work for it. In one sense the whole life of a preacher is an act of preparation for that moment when he stands in the pulpit. All of what he sees, all of what he hears, all of what he does, and all of what he is, work together to produce the healing, stimulating, guiding word he utters.

Sermons do not happen. They grow. They root in life, branch in experience, and blossom in that creative interplay of minds that is the ideal preacher-listener relationship. Creative thinking takes place when a pastor faces a problem with a genuine concern for its solution for himself and for his people. Though each man's work habits are different, there are certain essentials in the process. There must be time for quiet and thought. There must be an alertness to ideas and materials that can be used. There must be a creative moment when the thought and the materials begin to take a form that can make them useable.

One cannot reproduce the creative effort of others. One cannot give integrity to one's own message without creative effort. When Ernest Fremont Tittle stood in his pulpit one morning and told his people he could not preach the sermon he had announced because he hadn't gotten it to the place where he felt it was ready, he complimented his hearers and the whole Christian ministry. He affirmed a faith in a creative process that cannot always be made to conform to man-made schedules.

There are active psychological factors at work to aid the preacher in this creative process. Creativeness can be learned and stimulated. It is a psychological principle that we see what we want to see or are trained to see. Sight is a learned art. At an accident near our home recently, I saw this principle in action. The physician who arrived saw the injured persons and their needs because that was what he had been trained to see. The state policeman saw the relevant facts about the vehicles and their relation to each other. That was his special training. A maiden lady, who happened to be near by, saw blood and fainted. Each expressed an attitude by his action, and the attitude was conditioned by the cultivated process of seeing.

The preacher who has developed the habit of looking for new and fresh material that is actively related to the interests of his people will begin to see it cropping up here and there where he had not suspected it before. It may be in nursery rhymes, the daily paper, the *New Yorker,* the latest novel or a Broadway play. It may be in conversation, in the comments of a child or the sage wisdom of an older member of the parish. It may come through a new interpretation of the scriptures as an old familiar sentence takes on a new meaning because of other circumstances.

Seeing is a habit that can be cultivated. When we look for the new and fresh and meaningful, we begin to find it. So also is it true that hearing is a habit. A tape recording of a church service reveals a variety of noises that our habit of listening seems to screen out. People who live near a railroad get so they seldom hear the trains. Persons who live near the town clock may be kept awake by it when they first move there, but after a time they learn a habit of exclusive listening. They hear what they want to hear. This is also true of the preacher. He may develop good or bad habits of listening.

Recently I was given the New Testament on long-playing phonograph records. I have been hearing it with profit. I relax, close my eyes and try to open my mind to any new meanings that may come to me from the scriptures. It is interesting to note how the inflections, the emphases of another reader change the meaning at many points. The exercise in listening critically for new meanings and fresh insights seems to stimulate a response. Numerous texts suggest interesting possibilities. From the Gospel of Luke alone, I have jotted down over three hundred seeds of sermons. Jesus was defining the discipline of a creative impulse when he said, "Ask, and what you ask will be given you. Search, and you will find what you search for. Knock, and the door will open to you."

Each man's own genius will influence the nature of his creative habits. Sir W. M. Flinders Petrie, an Egyptologist of note, describes his method of work:

"I first assemble the material, state the problem as definitely as possible, and if no solution is evident, leave it alone. From time to time I may look over it to refresh my memory, but never to force a solution. After waiting days or years, I suddenly feel a wish to go over it again, and then everything runs smoothly and I can write without effort. There is unconscious growth of mind without perceptible effort in the interval."

Some ministers use a comparable method adapted to their need for a weekly creative effort. They use the summer vacation period to prepare a tentative outline for the year. This makes it possible to give balanced emphases and a constructive movement to the year's preaching. At the same time it gives this "unconscious growth of the mind" a chance to work for them.

Such a procedure can encourage the creative use of seeing and hearing. For months in advance the mind is alerted for any fresh or new material that can be used in the sermons scheduled. There is time to mull over ideas and accumulate a variety of material that one would not be able to find if the subject were approached with only a week's notice.

A minister of my acquaintance has a filing system for sermon material that has three parts, an incubator, a brooder, and sermons ready to serve. In the incubator he places seeds of ideas or scripture texts. From time to time he goes over the material to keep in mind what is there. When something is read or happens that might fit one of the germ ideas, he clips it to the starter sheet. When enough material has accumulated to give it body, he moves it along to the brooder. Here he watches it more closely, and adds or subtracts material as seems wise. Material in the brooder is drawn on for the year's program of preaching that he develops during his summer vacation. Such a program encourages the slow, sure development of worthwhile ideas, and at the same time discourages the frustrating search for material at the last minute as the hands of the clock snip off the minutes of Saturday evening.

Such a system of work can help to bring vital, fresh material into the sermons. Much poor preaching is a matter of habit. Poor preparation and poor material cannot produce a good result no matter how fine the delivery may be. If the preacher has a habit of late preparation and dependence upon old material or the material of others, he will seldom feel that sense of self-respect that comes with honest effort. He will be an exceptional actor if he does a convincing job in the pulpit.

It might be a good thing for a pastor to clear his files

periodically of all old material. A stretch of military service was helpful, for me, at two points. I got rid of about five hundred books that were a packing problem. I unloaded a few hundred pounds of accumulated file material. Both helped to free me from a past that was becoming constrictive. And a further incentive came with a weight limit of thirty pounds—maximum for Air Force personnel during wartime—for this meant cutting my library to a Bible, a book of worship and a few especially useful small pamphets. Yet it was possible to carry on a ministry, because I was compelled to draw from within myself those things that were of real experience and genuine witness, and also profit from those things about me that were new and a part of everyday life. The early itinerant preachers may have been so effective in building a church and ministering to a frontier because they had to depend only on what they could carry in their saddlebags and in their own hearts.

It is now possible, through mechanical aids, to approximate what Mr. Robert Burns might have had in mind had he penned (with my apologies),

> Ai, would some power the giftie gie us,
> To hear ourselves as ithers hear us.

It is a chastening experience to sit down with a tape recorder week after week and listen to a whole service from call-to-worship to benediction just as you did it. It is better to wait until after Sunday dinner. One should not be called on to hear himself on an empty stomach.

Some ministers have been put to sleep by their own sermons, via the tape recording. Others have been stabbed awake by shocking mannerisms and faulty construction. Such a method of listening gives a chance for a more objective evaluation. One can listen to the same sermon over and over; once for content, again for presentation, and again for such minutiae of public speech as repetitious words or exaggerated illustrations, or hackneyed phrases. Having heard with clarity, one can correct with candor and create with more courage.

Such creative listening can give the preacher a clearer idea of the movement of his sermons. He can sense the development of ideas and the effectiveness of his logic and the strength of his points. He can ask himself some questions and honestly answer them after listening to an accurate reproduction of what he does.

> Do ideas develop logically?
> Are points made with clarity?
> Is there extraneous and unimportant material?
> How could I improve the rate of speech?
> How could I bring more life and vitality to
> what I said?
> Did I close when I should have?
> Was presentation varied or monotonous?
> How would I rate the sermon if someone else
> preached it?

Speech that is too slow drags, and too rapid speech makes it difficult for hearers to follow. It is generally agreed that one hundred fifty words a minute is a good rate for public speech in the average sized church. Pauses between phrases should be brief, only a second or so, or the speech will begin to drag and appear broken up. Modulation of the voice can change the mood, and the rising inflection of a question, every so often, breaks the monotony of the falling inflection at the end of a sentence. In fact, practice at ending a sentence without a falling inflection is useful in general public speech.

Nothing is more deadly than the sepulchral tone assumed by some preachers, as if it were a necessary part of his professional equipment. It has the ring of insincerity, and violates the ideal of preaching as animated conversation. Almost as deadly are the mechanical gestures that distract attention from what is said. Radio broadcasting has proved that effective speech need not depend on gestures. But gestures can be useful. However, they are most effective when they are so natural a part of delivery that the speaker does not know he is gesturing and the listener is not distracted by them but rather feels that they are an unconscious supplement of speech itself.

Jesus probably spoke simply and directly. The fact that he sat down to speak indicates a practice of informality that invited people to come closer. The practice of pulpit harangues may explain why in many churches there is a premium on the back seats.

Next to poor delivery, perhaps nothing is more deadly than poor terminal facilities. This failing of the preacher has been dealt with in various ways by the wits. One said, "If you cannot strike oil in ten minutes, stop boring." Another said, "No souls are saved after twelve o'clock." But the length of a sermon is gauged not so much in minutes as in what it asks of those who listen. A fifteen-minute sermon may ask much of patience and good will. A forty-minute sermon may give much of inspiration and spiritual food with no demands upon the good nature of the listener. Perhaps we should make it a practice to err on the side of brevity rather than on the side of the listener's forbearance.

Drs. Laird and Laird suggest in their study of effective speech that one "quit talking while the listeners are still intensely interested, or quit when you have made a telling point. If you continue after either of these points, you will be making the same mistake as the manager who dragged in a batch of unfinished work at quitting time."

A man can have the personal prerequisites of a great preacher; he can have integrity and character, yet be ineffective in the pulpit. He can be good and devout and preach dull sermons. The ability to get attention and put the message across is of critical significance for effective preaching. To get attention sermons must relate to the interests of the people in a fresh way and concern genuine areas of life experience.

And a sermon must always have a conclusion. It moves toward an answer to a difficulty or toward a technique for meeting a problem. The listeners must know when that point is reached. Perhaps the sermon ends with a reassuring exhortation or with a simple word of encouragement. Perhaps it ends by a question that stimulates action on the part of the listener. Whichever it may be, there is need that the conclusion effectively tie together what has gone before so that the listener does not feel the frustration of being led toward spiritual food only to find it out of his reach.

Even the end of a sermon can be important in sustaining

attention; the way the preacher ends his sermon can make the listener want to hear what he has to say at another time. People do not have to go to church. The fact that they are there is a vote of confidence in the minister. He should not prove unworthy of such confidence.

2

COMMUNICATING THE WORD

*T*HE PREACHER is a communicator. That he has a special medium for communication is readily admitted. He does not operate with a simple use of language. He speaks with an authority granted by a tradition and a need. He communicates through a relationship supported by the mood of worship. All that takes place in public worship helps to sustain what he says in a form of communication that is both public and private.

But the atmosphere of the preacher's communication does not remove a responsibility for examining what takes place as a result. Preaching has long served a purpose. The response to it has verified a need. But no one has been quite sure either of the nature of the need or of the satisfaction of it. There has been a large measure of unexamined action.

Those who have examined the main emphases of some preachers have felt that the response was related to the content of the preaching, but there has been no simple or clear method of gauging the response of a congregation. Nor has there been a careful examination of the presuppositions upon which these types of preaching proceed.

Although I did not believe that any simple experiment could verify the response of listeners to a pulpit communication, I did feel that it might be possible to make some effective test of congregation response. So, with two aids, I attempted a form of examining group response under circumstances that were partially controlled. With anything as free as the service of public worship the controls would always have to be minimal.

Because the experiment did not seek to establish any particular findings (trying, rather, to establish the fact that a search for such findings would be feasible), it would be incorrect to attribute too much to what was observed. However, it is reasonable to assume that such an experiment can be a clue to both method and purpose, if any further examination of this form of communication were to be undertaken.

Three things were attempted.

First, a deliberate and carefully designed effort was made to use markedly different styles of sermonic approach to the congregation both as to content, method and purpose, and then observe the results of such differing types of communication.

Second, through the use of trained observers an effort was made to gauge the immediate response of the listeners to what was said.

Third, through the response of the congregation and its members over a period of several months, an effort was made to determine any significant delayed response to the communication that might become apparent.

However, there was a fourth response which though unanticipated was of the utmost importance. This was the reaction of individual members of the congregation to various types of message in relation to their particular personality needs and makeup.

The specific pulpit approach was to design and control a series of sixteen sermons in order to use group therapy forms—of necessity adapted to the preaching approach. For this purpose the repressive-inspirational method was alternated with what might be known as the analytic method.

The repressive-inspirational method as employed in group therapy would be characterized by a deliberate effort to repress the unpleasant and irritating in life and in its place emphasize the inspirational. This method has been employed with success by Alcoholics Anonymous. AA makes an effort to emphasize the group strength that can help alcoholics overcome their common difficulty by repressing the destructive urges of their appetite; at the same time, confidence and strength are inspired by dwelling on the power beyond themselves that sustains their efforts at control.

The main emphasis of Christian Science practice has been an employment of the repressive-inspirational technique. The evil, the unpleasant, the injurious is denied as unreal, and the pleasant, the healthful, and the creative is given a special place in thought and meditation.

Some preachers with a popular following, notably Dr. Norman Vincent Peale, have employed this method effectively in giving to their message a persistently inspirational quality while they repress many of the aspects of Christianity and life that could be construed as an unpleasant aspect of reality.

The repressive-inspirational method is particularly effective with an obsessive-compulsive type of personality which needs to be continually shored up or buttressed in order to face the onslaught of what it considers to be an unpleasant reality. The inner resources to sustain life are so weak that they must be supplemented by a regular ration of external support.

An illustration of the repressive-inspirational group therapy form as adapted to pulpit use is found in the following sermon resume:

Recapturing Self Confidence
"Come what may, I am confident." CORINTHIANS 5:6.
The loss of self-confidence weakens life. The inspired life finds the resources for confidence in all

circumstances. This is a subtle quality. It marks the difference between a baseball team that is losing and one that is playing inspired ball.

The message of a Bach arioso grows out of a life of tragedy, poverty, concern for twenty children, and rejected music, and it says Bach gained inner strength because he was given to the ideal of loving God and creating great music.

The inspired life is sustained by positive values. Nothing great is built on negatives. In personal terms this is shown in bereavement when people try to hold on to what they should willingly let go of. In social reform, the positive builds permanent results.

Hints to help recapture self-confidence:

Move from fears to folks, healthy human relations.

Move from guilt to guidance, seeking God's purpose for life.

Move from inhibitions to inspirations, seeking not the restraints on life, but its best freedom.

"If any man be in Christ Jesus, he is a new creature." This new life is no mystery. It is an achievement.

"Make me a captive, Lord, and then I shall be free, I sink in Life's alarms when by myself I stand.

My heart is weak and poor until its Master find, It has no spring of action sure, it varies with the wind.

Enslave it with thy matchless love, and deathless it shall reign.

My will is not my own 'til Thou hast made it Thine."

While this approach is effective with certain types of

personality needs, it is generally unacceptable to those who are able to meet reality with their own source of inner strength. They feel abused, cheated and deceived by an approach that denies any part of reality.

The analytic method makes a vigorous effort to explore openly the experience of life, to discover the inner resources that are available to deal with it realistically and competently. It avoids anything misleading. It believes in the innate capacity of each individual to deal with life's problems without escape and with candor.

In the religious context, this method was used by John Wesley in the small groups he organized for self-examination and spiritual growth. Also it has been used by the Oxford Group Movement as the basis for self-examination, self-criticism and self-improvement.

Traditionally it is the method that most closely resembles the prophets' stern criticisms and calls to repentance. Micah, Amos, and John the Baptist would have felt far more at home with the general mood of the analytic approach than they would with that of the repressive-inspirational.

The following resume shows the approach and content of the analytic type of sermon:

Conquering the Green-eyed Monster
"Thou shalt not covet" EXODUS 20:17.
One of the difficulties that causes economic, social and personal distress among us is the jealousy that is generated by the common practice of "keeping up with the Joneses." Let's face it and see what we can do about it.

From what source does the difficulty emerge? From

fear, insecurity, false standards for life and a lack of true love.

What can we do about it? Four suggested steps:

1. Admit it. As long as you keep fooling yourself by denial, nothing constructive can be done. A hard first step, but essential.

2. Analyze it. Let's take our jealousy apart and see what makes it tick. How did it start? Is it based on reality? Is it true or just? Is it a disease of our emotions? Be honest with ourselves.

3. Attack it. Let us use our best judgment, reason and candor to face this thing honestly and come to terms with it so our best self will have a chance to live. What are your true values and goals? If they are not good enough, now is the time to replace them. No one can do it but you yourself.

4. Abandon it. Start out with courage on a new course in life. Live beyond the small competitions, the small values, the small emotions. This may not be easy, but there is no easy way to pull yourself out of quicksand and get on firm ground. Are you aware of whom we are speaking? Are you willing to make the effort?

You do not stand alone. The power of the Christian faith sustains you in your quest for life's true values. But it places the burden squarely on your shoulders. Little values produce trivial lives. True values produce heroic lives. Which would you have?

Some effective modern preachers have employed this method to keep their hearers alert to responsibility and to prevent the mood of complacency. Usually such preachers attract the competent, assured type of personality who seeks stimulation for a more carefully examined and useful life.

But because congregations tend to be made up of more than one type of personality it may be important for the preacher to employ a change of pace that will at one time "Comfort the afflicted" and at other times "Afflict the comfortable." Yet even here it is important to have some idea of what is being done, how it is being achieved, and what the effect is upon those for whom the message is not especially relevant.

In the experiment under discussion, and one hesitates to speak of a series of sermons as experiments even though a measure of honesty makes us aware of the experimental nature of most preaching, a definite effort was made to give every other sermon the repressive-inspirational emphasis and alternate sermons the analytic tone.

In the repressive-inspirational sermons the material was exclusively positive and optimistic. The illustrations dwelt on the heroic in life. Questions were not thrown in people's faces, but affirmations were stressed. Inspirational ideas and inspirational poetry were freely utilized. When the sermons approached their conclusions, no sense of self-conscious introspection was employed, but rather an outgoing feeling of good will and acceptance, and each point was sealed with a bit of scripture or inspirational poetry.

In the analytical sermons a searching look was taken into life and its meaning with the burden of responsibility for acts and attitudes placed squarely upon man. The measuring stick of the person of Christ was held up clearly as the ultimate guide in adequate living. The listeners were urged to look in upon their lives with a concern for correction, a desire to lead a new life with the help of the religious resources available to them.

The sermons were bristling with the kind of questions that threw them back upon themselves in self-examination. While no doubt was expressed of their ability to handle the problems of life, neither was there any doubt as to their individual responsibilities. The emphasis was short on inspiration and long on self-awareness as a first premise for learning to live a new and better life.

Until one sets such a disciplined and exclusive theme in a sermon, he does not realize how usual it is for a sermon to include both points of view. Though the test we made may not have been entirely successful, a sincere effort was made for the duration of this series of sermons, to keep the content and method clearly related to the group therapy approach that was being evaluated.

I, myself, had been trained in evaluating the response of the group both by many years of practice and also by special work in the Study of Group Procedures as taught by Prof. Kenneth Herrold at Columbia University. But as support to my own observations, I had two well qualified and competent observers. One was Prof. Wellman J. Warner, head of the Department of Sociology at the Graduate School of Arts and Sciences at New York University, President of the International Congress of Group Psychotherapy, and President of the Board of the Moreno Institute, where much significant work in the field of group work has been done. The other was Prof. Frank Rathbone, Doctor of Education and on the faculty of Brooklyn College. In addition to their formal training in these fields, Dr. Warner is an ordained clergyman, and Dr. Rathbone is a lay preacher who has served a parish in Connecticut.

The observers made no direct inquiry concerning the sermons or the reactions of the listeners to them. The method employed was to observe with care the congregational reaction during the preaching of the sermon, to listen to such comments as were made after the sermons, and to evaluate the response as it could be gauged by experienced observers through verbal, facial, and other mannerisms or responses. The observers were regular worshippers at this church and so were better able to compare any reactions to what might be considered a norm over a much longer period of time.

That there was a difference in response was immediately clear to all three observers. (It must be kept in mind that apart from the three observers no one else was aware of the fact that such an experiment was in progress.)

While the repressive-inspirational sermons were being preached, there was a comfortable, relaxed feeling evident in the congregation. There was a ready and willing response. The members of the group seemed to be participating as a group who were bound together in a mood of pleasure and confidence, and there was little or no coughing.

This was made explicit in responses after the service. Numerous comments were made to the pastor, of which the following are samples. "Your sermon was so helpful this morning." "You said just what I needed to hear." "That was a helpful sermon this morning." "Now I feel set for the next week. Thank you." "That was a lovely sermon." "You ought to have that sermon printed so I can read it every day." "When I came to church this morning, I felt down; now I feel up." "We need more sermons like that." It seemed interesting how much of his state of mind a listener could reveal in one short sentence.

It was highly significant to the pastor that during the weeks following the repressive-inspirational sermons, except for situational factors that had no relation to the sermon, there were no counseling relations established. This may or may not have been good, and we made no effort to evaluate it at this point. There is evidently a type of preaching that can so satisfy emotional needs, at least temporarily, that persons either do not need or will not seek aid in coming to grips with them.

The response following the analytic sermons was quite a contrast. The observers felt a marked difference in the mood of the congregation while listening. While there was no less attention, there was a different quality of response. The group seemed to be broken up into individuals as questions were asked that had to be dealt with on individual terms. The feeling of identity as a group was at least partially lost. The sense of joy and responsiveness was replaced by a mood of introspection and uncomfortable self-examination. This was verified by the preacher who felt less response and almost a mood of antagonism as if the listeners had come for one thing and were given something else.

One of the interesting responses that came from examining the tape recordings of the services was found in the degree of coughing. Coughing is about the only acceptable method available for members of a congregation to express displeasure, defense, or rejection. Perhaps it is done unconsciously, as a rejection of discomfort or irritation. Perhaps it is consciously done as a type of noise that temporarily blots out the words that are uncomfortable. The season of the year was the same for both types of sermons, but the mood of discomfort and rejection was revealed by much more coughing during the analytical than during the repressive-inspirational sermons.

This mood was reflected after the service, for the listeners had little to say. A few remarks like, "You were talking straight at me this morning," or "That was a thoughtful sermon," were mixed with vague comments about the weather. The look in the eyes of those who went out was questioning, as if they had come seeking bread and were handed a stone. While the congregation usually gathered on the lawn outside the church for friendly chats after the service, there seemed to be less of this after the analytical sermons, as if the mood were more restrained and people felt more concerned about themselves as persons than as parts of a sharing group.

Probably the most significant reaction observed after the analytic sermons was the instituting of pastoral counseling relationships. During the eight weeks that followed the analytic type of sermon, over two hundred hours of pastoral counseling were begun. The largest single response was following a sermon dealing with jealousy. On Sunday afternoon and on Monday there were numerous requests for interviews. Since the sermon itself seemed no more effective than others in the series one had to conclude that it was its theme which struck home.

Toward the end of the four months' series there was evidence of an attendance response, although other factors were undoubtedly involved and no weight could be attached to the fact that more persons seemed to attend on the Sundays when the repressive-inspirational sermons were being preached.

However, quite by chance a comment came to one of the observers that seemed quite significant. In speaking to a new neighbor who had moved into the community, Dr. Warner invited her to church. Her response was, "Is it true that your pastor preaches a good sermon only every other Sunday?" In response to further questioning, Dr. Warner learned that another neighbor who had been in psychotherapy as an obsessive-compulsive neurotic had invited the new neighbor to church but had given the friendly warning, based on her own need, that a good sermon was to be expected only every other Sunday. Here the specific response of one type of personality to one type of sermon was clearly shown. How often this sort of thing determines the response of members of the parish to the message of their pastor is beyond calculation, but it may well be more important than we have imagined.

I indicated at the beginning that it would be unwise to attribute to this brief experiment more than was warranted. However, it does seem to indicate that the content and method employed, if it is related to certain known procedures as far as group response is concerned, can be expected to produce results not unlike those that might be expected in other controlled circumstances.

It is also fairly evident that the response of the congregation differs in response to differing methods of approach, even though it would be hard to establish any dependable form of measurement.

It is also fairly clear that one type of sermon leads to one type of delayed action while another type gets a far more specific and significant delayed reaction.

Even though we may not realize it, it is safe to say that the type of personality, and the problems that the person brings with him to church, in large measure determine the response to any specific type of pulpit presentation. If this presentation were to be continued indefinitely, it would probably account for a winnowing process, whereby one group would remain where they could get what they consciously or unconsciously needed, while the rest would go elsewhere in search of what their needs dictated. Or as might be the case in some denominations, they would seek a change in pastors feeling that in some such way they would satisfy the needs of their souls.

If such a simply designed experiment with preaching indicates a clear direction, it is reasonable to assume that a more careful and detailed study of what takes place in the communication between pulpit and pew would be more profitable. Certainly any medium that employs as many persons as often as preaching communication does is worthy of careful study and examination.

Perhaps two general observations would be worthy of more careful exploration. First, preaching, whether or not we are willing to admit it, is essentially an art form, where a great idea is formed into artful expression through the impact of a competent personality upon an established medium. This definition tends to eliminate at once those who are in the practice stages of handling the medium and getting the idea. Also it makes clear that the practice of preaching invariably employs the medium with the desire to communicate to listeners the important idea.

This concept of preaching stresses the role of the preacher as the creator in the employment of an art form. His own personality is then inseparably bound up with what is communicated.

The second general observation is that something about the exchange that takes place in preaching may modify the relation of the individual to the group. The lonely and distressed person may be integrated into a group through the words that are spoken to the group. The development of common feelings and desires may be so clearly a group reaction that the members share the emotional response and are bound together in it. This feeling of identity and group relationship may be an important factor in helping to give stability and balance to the disturbed individual.

But the process may work another way. The type of pulpit communication may be such that it breaks the group up into individuals so that the strength of identity is lost and the individuals feel alone, and conscious of their need for help to move beyond their loneliness. Here is where the door may be opened to counseling. But it is well to ask whether or not the practice employed to stimulate the response is warranted. Much that we accept as an evidence of successful response to our pulpit communication may be little more than the projection of elements of our own personality through a medium which communicates but also, on occasion, manipulates.

The preacher on Sunday morning is a communicator. What he communicates is an extension of himself. The quality of his message and the methods he employs may be consciously or unconsciously the devices for satisfying his own important personal needs. So the aggressive pastor may use the pulpit to flay his people, while the empathetic pastor moves into their thoughts and feelings with a desire to bring peace and comfort as well as helpful insight. The goals may be the same, yet the methods vary.

If this rather simple experimental observation reveals anything, it is that more is happening in the relationship of pulpit and pew than we have been apt to believe. Persons are involved in a method of relationship as well as in the content of a message. The emotional needs of the preacher may well be the major factor in qualifying the relationship that emerges between speaker and listener. While the pastor has a privileged position in speaking to his people both by tradition and by status, he cannot press this privilege too far without results pro or con. Persistently injured persons will tend to move away from his aggressive assaults. Or they may be drawn by his empathetic projection of himself. Those seeking intellectual stimulation will move in one direction while those who seek a father figure may move in another.

More than we dare believe, preaching is a vital force, affecting life and creating response. Often the response is more significant than would be measured by a few words uttered by listeners after a service. Something important can take place in preaching. It is tragic when such a rich opportunity is wasted. It is rewarding when life-changing forces are set in motion.

3

ACHIEVING IDENTITY

THE ESSENTIAL TASK of the minister is that of mediating God's power and love and mercy through a capacity for soul-communion that manifests itself through both preaching and pastoral care.

If the minister is what we like to call "effective," this

is usually the result, consciously or unconsciously, of a sensitivity on his part to the needs of people and to the resources of the Creator. He is a believer in spiritual power, and because he believes, he lives his belief. And because he lives his belief people feel the genuineness of his ministry. His power as mediator is not given him as an act of ordination. Rather it is the unconscious compliment his people pay him when they become convinced that, through him, their soul-needs can be satisfied.

The capacity for sensitivity, the ability to feel with and for his people, is a pastor's supreme art. It means he sees not himself, but beyond himself. It means he sees the multitude but not as a multitude. Rather, he is sensitive to the multitude as the group of individual souls, each valuable in himself, for the soul must always of its nature be individual.

The preacher who is able to move into the thought and feeling of his people, who is able to achieve identity with them, creates the mood for effective interchange. In any relationship where there is no chance to talk back, a special atmosphere must be created wherein persons can *feel* back.

This capacity to identify can be developed in many ways. Through all the things the pastor sees, feels, reads and experiences he opens doors of understanding. This is not accidental. It is a discipline of life, to live in the beyond-self, in the life and thought of the people he serves. Let us think of some of the ways for doing this.

It is significant that the Gospel writer as he approached the task of presenting those important utterances of Jesus called the "Sermon on the Mount," framed the sermon in informal and personal terms. Jesus was seated informally on a mountainside close to people, not formally in a synagogue. His approach to the people was that of "seeing the multitude." How important both for preaching and the counseling relationship is the ability to see others as they are, and in terms of their own needs, a personalized group.

This capacity to see others is not accidental or automatic. It is a learned process. It is an achievement. Perhaps it is best called an art.

Even in the physical realm this is true of seeing. For there is both a structure and a process of seeing. The structure may be inherited but the process is developed.

The human eye is by its nature an especially sensitized area of skin tissue that has, through a long process of development, become sensitive to the variations of light rays as they are reflected on a variety of surfaces and textures. The human eye is, as it were, a minute camera with amazing mechanical capacities.

This minute camera is able to take still pictures or pictures in rapid motion. It is able to take pictures in full color or in black and white. It has a capacity for instantaneous development. It never needs to be reloaded, and it can focus automatically at various light intensities and distances. It has built-in light meters and filters, so that it can see a drop of rain on the end of your nose or a star a million light-years away.

Yet all of that amazing structure would be useless unless one knew how to use it—that is, learned the discipline of sight. Here a psychological principle is at work. Through a long period of experimentation and development there emerges an intricate pattern of associations that gives meaning to the flow of light waves.

If you watch a young child, you will see this process as it is developed. The child at first has no sense of depth or perspective. In order to develop it, he combines touch with sight. Everything he sees must be felt and handled. Learning to see depth causes many broken objects, but where else is so priceless an art learned so inexpensively?

Working diligently for ten or twelve hours a day, the child is able in the period of two or three years to develop his sense of association and meaning and depth so that he can evaluate objects without touching them. Rapidly moving, high intensity light-waves are, through a process of organization, invested with meaning. What an achievement of the human mind it is when the child is able to say at last, "Look at the beautiful flower."

Perhaps one of the great miracles of life is the ability of a person to look at a bouquet of variously colored flowers, and so organize the variety of light-ray speeds as to be able to see and enjoy the beauty of the flowers. Just think of the discipline that is involved in looking at a many-colored picture with its demand for organization, association and investment of meaning. Here is an illustration of how a piece of equipment, the ounce or so of fluid, nerve and tissues that we call the eye, can be given a new significance by a long and tediously acquired discipline.

Yet even that discipline is intensely personal and so conditioned by the experience and intake of the mental life that it reveals our own inner capacity. Our emotional and intellectual pre-conditioning is itself a definite part of seeing. For how we use the equipment largely determines how we are able to use it.

The minister is a specialist in seeing people. He is the product of a discipline that makes him sensitive to people's needs. Through years of training and experience he has developed the capacity to bridge the gap of otherness, and make himself at one with the needs, trials and sufferings of his people.

People are for him not just so many bodies that fill the pews. They are not empty vessels into which he pours his wisdom. They are living, struggling souls who come seeking a light.

Again and again our Master revealed the importance of this sensitivity of soul. He saw the invisible. He heard the inaudible. He saw the multitude in all its complexity and individuality before he opened his mouth to preach. He indicated that his disciples were custodians of a privilege to help others "to see those things that you see . . . and to hear those things that you hear."

If the minister is the exponent of the fine art of seeing people, how does he go about the task of perfecting this art? What are the tools of his insight? What are the open doors to this understanding? How can his eyes become eyes of compassion? How does his soul become a communing instrument, both with God and with his people?

It is important not to disregard a certain intuitive sense that is one characteristic of a good pastor. Dangerous as it may be to depend on anything as capricious as intuition when it stands alone, it is equally unwise to ignore the sum-total response of a carefully disciplined personality to those spiritual overtones that might be called super-normal. Jesus had a capacity to see into people with his whole being. Many of his devoted followers have found that genuine love and compassion led to a communion of souls and an insight into deeper needs that was hardly indicated by superficial observation.

While this intuitive capacity of the sensitive pastor is not to be disregarded, it is wise to use it against a background of the best possible understanding of the dynamics of the human personality, and the illnesses of the human soul. While the Christian pastor is careful not to block the channels through which the powers of the Holy Spirit may flow, he does not presume on any peculiar powers of his own to take liberties with the soul of another. While the Christian pastor would not deny those insights and sensitivities that prayer can give, he would not want to ask of prayer what is both unreasonable and unworthy. For prayer and insight are resources of the wise and diligent, rather than shortcuts for the lazy and unprepared.

It is wise to remember that the total response of the personality is built upon the accumulation of preparation and experience that have gone into the training of the person. Nothing in this connection would prove to be more useful than the intuitive judgment of a wise and balanced servant of God. Nothing would seem to be more unfortunate than the imprudent use of intuition by the unwise and unbalanced neophyte or charlatan of the religious association.

Definite supplemental sources of aid in the developing of the pastor's art of "seeing people" are available to all. Invariably, the masters of understanding have been immersed in the great literature of the past. Jesus had at his disposal the books of poetry, law and prophesy of the Jewish tradition. Paul knew not only the Jewish literature but was conversant with the literature of the Graeco-Roman world as well.

One can find in the words of the great poets not only the honest and perspicacious expression of human feeling but also the most choice, economical and graphic form of utterance. John Donne says of the ministry in a few lines what many pages might struggle and fail to say.

> What function is so noble as to be
> Ambassador to God and destiny?
> To open life! to give kingdoms to more
> Than kings give dignities? to keep heaven's door?
> Mary's prerogative was to bear Christ, so
> 'Tis preacher's to convey him, for they do,
> As angels out of clouds, from pulpits speak,
> And bless the poor beneath, the lame, the weak.

Where in a sermon on social injustice could the displeasure of God at the forces that blight men's personalities be brought to finer focus and more vigorous expression than in these few words of that rebel soul, William Blake?

> And did the Countenance Divine
> Shine forth upon our clouded hills?
> And was Jerusalem builded here
> Among these dark Satanic Mills?

How better would one be able to bring the majesty and mystery of the Incarnation into the language and mood of

common man than these chaste and chastening words of
Harry Webb Farrington?

> I knew not how that Bethlehem's Babe
> Could in the Godhead be,
> I only know the Manger's Child
> Has brought God's Love to me.

One cannot read such an expression of faith in the soul
of man as Carl Sandburg's *The People, Yes*, without gain-
ing a new insight into one's self and every other man. For
here is the type of integrity of vision and depth of insight
that undergirds the judgment upon which a dependable
intuitive sense can be built.

Nor does one ignore the great dramatists when the windows into the human soul are explored. In sharper relief
than we have ever dared accept, an ancient Greek play-
wright, Sophocles, made the most elusive of human emotions stand up and walk about the stage. In his *Oedipus
Rex, Oedipus at Colonus* and *Antigone*, he presents the
struggle of the personality as it seeks to grow into emotional
maturity in spite of the compulsions of childhood's attach-
ments.

No student of the human soul has finished his studies
until he shares with Shakespeare his understanding of the
intensity of the inner battle that takes place when man is
faced with moral choices and immoral urges. For not only
the struggle becomes a live and vibrant thing before his eyes,
but just as real are the consequences of moral choice that
come marching upon the stage.

The novelists and allegorists like Dostoevski and Bunyan are rich sources of understanding of the complexity of the drives and forces that work upon the human soul as he seeks to find his religious destiny. And where could one find a more searching look at the sources of human suffering than in Miguel de Unamuno's *The Tragic Sense of Life?* These are the raw materials out of which the student of life builds his understanding of the depth and complexity of the struggles of the soul to find its meaning.

Perhaps no source of study is more revealing than biography and autobiography, for here we are able to deal with the original and unvarnished source material of life itself. Here we can sense the interplay of life with its environment. Here we can see the personality moulded, warped, or strengthened by the inter-play of material and spiritual forces.

One lays aside the *Life and Letters of Charles Darwin* with a feeling that here was a fine and gentle soul who allowed something rich within him to be stifled by the deadening discipline of the scientific method. Sabatier's fine life of St. Francis, on the other hand, indicates the capacity of a soul to grow when soul growth becomes the one central and conscious goal of living.

The intimate familiarity with quite different types of personality that biographical material affords helps to furnish the mind with a consciousness of the qualities of being that are present in those with whom we continually work. For every man has within his makeup a little bit of every other man, and until we see the possibilities of this varied expression of his nature we cannot do him justice. Where is the person who has not felt an urge for withdrawal such as that which sent Henry David Thoreau to Walden Pond? Or where is the pastor who has not been reassured by coming across those words in John Wesley's Journal that indicate that he would often preach a sermon on faith when he found his own faith was failing? This is the stuff life is made of, and no man who works with people can have too much of it built into the sub-structure of his thinking.

Probably one of the richest sources of understanding of the human personality in our day is the psychological insight that has come through the scientific study of human nature. The last fifty years have produced a staggering amount of information, much of it unrelated to the pastor's work and even more of it undigested as far as any over-all philosophy of life is concerned. But the study of the personality and its reactions in the laboratory have given sound understanding of the personality as it operates out of the laboratory, and there is where the pastor's concern becomes operative.

The pastor who is well equipped should have fairly well in mind, and available for ready reference, some of the standard texts in the field of psychology and psychiatry. He should seek for himself and his work the findings of such contemporaries as Jung, Fromm, Horney, Hock, Alexander and Dunbar, as well as the more specifically religious writings of Weatherhead, May, Burkhart, Dicks and Fosdick. No one of these persons is able to represent all of the valuable trends of thought in such a rapidly developing field of research, but each has his contribution to make and the pastor wants to be aware of it.

The danger that is ever present, however, is that any

one point of view might become determinative in the approach of the pastor. The pastor is not the exponent of any one psychological discipline, for he is obliged to evaluate all such disciplines by one that is more demanding—a spiritual discipline that sees the person not as subject to limited and limiting forces, but as responsive to unlimited spiritual possibilities. The pastor uses psychological insight as an aid in his spiritual discipline. He does not allow himself to become the servant of any minor discipline, useful as it may be in his pastoral work.

His study of the psychological and psychiatric literature of his day makes it possible for the pastor to see other souls with love and concern plus a capacity for analysis and interpretation that will assist him in his role as a soul healer. His understanding of the growth process makes it possible for him to see and interpret the evidences of immaturity that reveal a flaw in the personality's balanced rate of maturation. This will make him a wiser interpreter of those defenses with which the personality protects itself. And when the inner conflicts bring about an acute malfunction of the personality, he is wise enough to interpret it not in moral terms but in terms of the soul illness that predicates the behavior that is often called immoral.

The pastor's study of psychodynamics and psychopathology makes it possible for him to interpret the behavior of others not as a personal affront, but rather as a symptom of the deeper soul needs which it is his mission to satisfy. I well remember the occasion early in my ministry when I found reassurance and understanding in the words of a wise professor, Rollin Walker, who said to a group of future ministers, "Remember that one of your functions will be to serve as an instrument to draw off the venom of sick souls." One day for three hours and twenty minutes a sorely disturbed woman whose husband had died told me what she thought of me and my ministry. During that time there was not a kind or appreciative word to assuage the bitterness of her denunciation. Yet those words of the wise professor made it easy for me to listen to her soul's need rather than to her words, and thus open the door for a ministry of helpfulness.

The pastor operates in the most demanding of laboratories, the laboratory of life. Any psychological insight that he may have is made immediately operative in the realm of actual people and their problems. On Sunday morning he sees injured and frightened souls looking to him for a word of understanding and helpfulness. They come, aware of life in the commonplace but wanting to find life in its promised abundance. The master of the art of seeing would keep his eyes on his Master, who used similar opportunities so effectively. He took the commonplace situations of life and filled them with a new meaning. He was able to dramatize problems in brief narratives so that the people could see their problems walk before them. When they were able to see relationships objectively, they were able to think through their problems. Through this process they felt their burdens strangely eased. They went on their way with new hope, new courage, and a new sense of purpose because they had found a new relationship with their God. Jesus, the master of insight, helped them to see themselves as they were.

Sometimes our people almost cry out to be seen as they

are, and we look beyond them to some unreal and manufactured idea of a person. If we preach to that unreal being,
we can be sure that we have little contact with those who sit
longingly before us. How do people want to be seen? What
do they bring to church with them, and what do they hope to
take away?

A questionnaire, seeking answers at this level, queried the
man in the pew. The purpose was to find out what people
want from their pastors through their sermon. About half
of the four thousand queried indicated a concern about
intensely personal matters, such as the futility of life, insecurity in personal relations, a haunting sense of loneliness, problems that involve marriage and the proper control
of the sex drives, the effect of alcohol, false ideas of religion
and morals, a feeling of inferiority, the problem of suffering as well as the problems of illness, and the feelings of
guilt and frustration.

Another fourth of those who responded were concerned
about family problems, parenthood and child training, in-
fidelity, religious differences, and other problems that were
symptoms of tensions in human relations. The remainder
and relatively small minority were concerned about social,
community and the more traditional religious problems.

So the man in the pew indicated by an overwhelming
percentage that his problems were those that grow out of
immaturity, inner conflict, and aggressive behavior. His
were the problems of making himself a fit person to live
with. He wanted to know how to grow into this abundant
life that the church talks about. He came seeking bread.
How often did he receive a stone?

Ian MacLaren, the eminent Scotch preacher, speaking

to a group of young ministers said this, "Remember, everyone is having a difficult time." Some may be wearing their hearts on their sleeves while others may be drawing heavily on their courage to present a brave front to the world. But life is not easy and a compassionate concern for the struggle of all men is an important part of the equipment of a helpful pastor. Part of this matter of "seeing the invisible" is to be able to look beyond the crust of life, the exteriors that men carefully build about themselves, to the deep inner areas of life where need is great and where the resources of religion are vital for life.

From a group of sociological and psychiatric sources we can get some statistical information that may help us to see our people not as they want to be seen but as they are. For some reason people seem inclined to present their best side to their minister. But he does not understand their needs until he is able to see the worst as well as the best. It may be helpful to know that, in all probability, twenty out of every hundred of our people have been so recently bereaved in family or close circle of friends that they are seriously concerned about their personal loss and the whole matter of life, death and immortality.

Of each hundred, there are thirty-three who have problems of adjustment in marriage and home life serious enough to make deep inroads on their happiness. Probably half have problems of emotional adjustment at home, in school, at work or in the community that seriously impair their efficiency and affect their happiness. Twenty in the hundred are contending with neuroses that may range all the way from alcohol addiction to obsessive behavior and neurotic anxiety. From three to eight are struggling against the sense of guilt and social ostracism that comes with homosexual impulses.

Because misery seems to love company, and the problems of the emotionally disturbed are "legion," many persons are trying to keep life going in the face of a combination of forces that are destructive to peace of mind and their general welfare. They are in the congregation on Sunday morning, and they need to be seen. The pastor who prepares for Sunday with a consciousness of the needs of his people is a vastly different person in the pulpit from the charming soul who makes a Sabbath descent from his ivory tower to soliloquize with and about the unreal in himself and those who hear him.

Jesus "saw the multitude" and made individuals of them. He could take the person who lived in a world of crowds with its particular type of loneliness and make him feel that he was a creature of significance in the eyes of God, and therefore in his own eyes and the eyes of others. He could take the aged with their fears and make them feel that life was a beginning, not an end. He could take the youth and lead their turbulent emotions to a dedication that gave all to follow him. And with a keen sense of understanding, he saw the chains of slavery and fear that breed the temptations of those middle years which can be so rich or so poor. In some fine and meaningful way he could look at a multitude of people as if he were a shepherd, and see them as his sheep.

The word "Pastor" in its best meaning indicates this ability of the minister to see his people as if they were his souls "to make them thine." His is no unreal blind-eye view of life and people. He sees them for what they are, but he is a custodian of a saving faith. He sees and understands the worst, but he also seeks and understands the best. He sees life, and he sees it whole, and part of that wholeness is a saving grace that can bring new life.

There is no way of getting closer to persons than to share the experience of their day-by-day living. In the small parish, the minister can help with the haying. He can move in and out of the major concerns of home and community life almost like a member of the family. This is not done so easily in urban districts, but even here the pastor can find ways to work with and play with members of the parish at the times when the more formal relationships of life are not as necessary.

When Evelyn Underhill was having difficulty in her spiritual life, she wrote to Baron Von Hugel, a guide of deep spiritual discernment in matters of the soul's life, and he advised her to spend less time in spiritual retreats and give more time to real people. He urged her to visit twice a week in the homes of the impoverished, to see their condition and feel their feelings.

The minister who walks close with his people during the week, who identifies his life with their daily interests, has no difficulty on Sunday in speaking so that the listener in the pew knows what he means. The illustrations that come walking out of life do not have to be interpreted, for they interpret themselves. The person-consciousness that feels the feelings of the listener, has already achieved an identity that cannot be manufactured in flights of unreal fancy.

Even if a close relationship with members of the parish does not always furnish the ideal illustration for the Sunday sermon, it establishes a bridge of human relationships across which the mind can more easily walk back and forth. The preacher in his close identity with the listener becomes more of a person himself. He is not a mere professional employer of words; he is a friend talking, and the response, though silent, is none the less real.

The pastor stands before his people, not to condemn, not to judge, not to punish, but to see with the eye of the mind and the soul, and having seen, to help others to see.

In these days of specialization, the minister's great art and much needed specialty is to see all of the person, so that he may see himself for all that he is. For when a man sees all that he is he sees his relationship to God. The pastor who can see God and see man can help bring them together. He can make God real and near to those who come seeking Him, not in the abstract, but in the revelation of a power which can bring them "newness of life."

Don Marquis, in his little book called *Poems and Portraits,* expresses in final form the function of the preacher as he approaches his people:

Out of agonies and love shall God be made,
He is wrought of cries that meet between the worlds.
Of seeking cries that have come forth from the cruel
    spheres to find a God and be stilled.
For he builds himself of the passion of martyrs,

And he is woven in the ecstasy of great lovers,
And he is wrought of the anguish of them that have
greatly needed him.

The preacher who does not feel that his message is wrought with a consciousness of the "anguish of those that have greatly needed him" has only partly heard the call to preach.

As we drink deeply of the insight and spirit of the words of the Sermon on the Mount, let us not forget those important words, and that more important mood, that so characterized the approach of our Master to those who came to hear him.

"And seeing the multitude . . . he opened his mouth and taught them. . . ."

4

THE FRAMEWORK OF PREACHING

A T THE BEGINNING we said that preaching was a special type of communication because it carried an authority of tradition and because it was framed in a service of worship.

Part of the authority of tradition is inherited and part is remade in each generation according to its own needs.

We have looked at the authority Jesus gave to preaching through his understanding of human needs and his concern for the welfare of souls. We have looked at the authority that may be achieved by the preacher who is able to identify with the needs and aspirations of his people by seeing them as people rather than as a multitude.

Let us look now at the framework within which the pulpit effort is made. In response to basic needs, the service of worship has employed several forms of communication that tend to supplement and emphasize what may be said in the sermon.

There are basic art forms that stimulate kinesthetic responses within the person. There is the strong influence of architecture, for who can resist the strong upward pull of towering Gothic arches even though no words are spoken?

There is the stimulating effect of music in the many forms in which it is employed in worship, from carillon to organ to blended human voices.

There is the rhythmic stimulation of the dance as employed in the stately religious processional. This may be emphasized throughout a service where every act and movement is done with precision and dignity.

There is also the added dimension in communication that comes through prayer where in silence or in audible expression the relation between the Creator and the creature is brought into sharp focus.

There is a difference between reading and speaking. The service of worship also affords an opportunity for the response that comes through the reading of the historic words that have long been the rallying point for those who seek God and seek to be known by God.

Also in worship there is a place for the creative use of silence which may become an active and stimulating form of communication.

Even the benediction as a traditional form of blessing may have important therapeutic values if it is properly understood.

When the sermon, with its clearly defined function, is set in such a framework of other types of communication, it ceases to be a mere speech. It becomes something more. Let us try to examine what the rest of the service does for the sermon and also the responsibility of the sermon to the rest of the service.

Perhaps there are few places where the unconscious power of basic human needs is more clearly at work than in the very nature and content of a service of worship. Though the forms may vary, certain essentials persist. These persistent elements employ art forms that relate primitive needs at the emotional level with the achievement of artistic competence at the intellectual level.

This artistic competence is achieved in proportion to the degree of success acquired in meeting basic needs. These needs are so complete an amalgamation of the emotional and the intellectual, the spiritual and the physical that they can only be satisfied in a situation where the "organism as a whole" is approached. Often, this can happen only when there is an unexamined atmosphere. When too critical or analytic an attitude is allowed to intrude, the mood is broken. In any art, technique, while important, must be secondary to the artistic fulfillment.

In the great art of living the framework of worship can meet several important needs. These needs are all essential for spiritual and emotional health. There is perspective, a capacity to accept and appreciate, an ability to see one's self as he is, an undergirding faith, a drive toward creative spiritual activity, and a feeling of the worth of life itself. "Art penetrates man's senses and arouses emotions, feelings, the glands and intellect. It affects his entire past, his rites, his ceremonies, his religion, his morale and his conduct.

"Although the arts have never been seriously mobilized for therapeutic attacks as have herbs, chemicals, electricity and numerous others agents, yet they made themselves keenly felt in the fields of mental hygiene and as useful social vitamins."[1] And perhaps nowhere has this been more evident than in the forms of group psychotherapy that developed long before persons were conscious of the fact that such was their function. When life is disrupted and out of focus, a steady diet of spiritual vitamins can help to maintain right relationships.

Worship can bring to life a healing perspective. The outlook on life can be determined by the way we look at things. This is shown in the contrasting ideas of perspective in Oriental and Western art. The Oriental mind is more subjective, is relatively indifferent to time and space, more concerned with abstract forms and colors and ideas. As a result, Oriental painting is apt to have a wandering perspective with several horizons. Lines of perspective, instead of meeting in the distance, are apt to meet in the foreground. What is true of painting is also more or less true of the Oriental concern for those things that reveal *subjective* values like tradition, courtesy and ancestry.

The Western view of life is quite the contrary and its effect upon art is obvious. There is a strong consciousness of the objective, with sharply defined horizons, and a firm sense of objects and object relationships. Perspective lines start in the foreground and run toward a focal point in the dim distance. Time and space are the realities, and the subjective has little or no place in the traditional art forms of the Western world.

The human spirit and its emotional counterpart, however, are never completely satisfied with an either-or approach to perspective. The human body lives in space-time relationships, but the human spirit dwells among values that are not measured. The need of worship moves beyond the frustration of the either-or, and lets the human spirit dwell in the two realms which life has destined for it. In so doing it helps to restore to life the balance that might not otherwise exist.

Perspective can take the immediate problem that seems so overwhelming and place it in a context where it is seen differently. Today's newspaper can be a frightening experience with no sense of perspective, but a month-old newspaper seems strangely flat and uninteresting. If the vantage point afforded by a month's time can work such a change, what can a contemplation of eternal values do?

Worship can also bring a healing quality of appreciation to life. In business it is routine to figure both profit and loss, but in the matter of life there are many who count only the loss. With a gruesome, pessimistic and unappreciative view of life they see only the miserable and unhappy. Such a view of life only aggravates the unpleasant and multiplies the unfortunate.

The act of giving thanks helps to bring life back into balance by weighing the blessings against the misfortunes. Though no life is free of its disturbances, there are multitudes of things and people and happenings for which one can be truly thankful. We need the reality to see life as it is and not as it may seem to be. That person who finds no opportunity for thankfulness is neither fair to himself nor to life in general when he begins to count his misfortunes. That person who has learned the art of thankfulness learns life's quiet satisfactions, and finds a balance that tends to discount anything that would destroy right relations with his Creator.

Worship also brings a healing self-sight. One of life's difficult problems is to see ourselves as we are. A trick of the mind used by neurotic personalities to protect themselves from coming face to face with themselves is to deal in opposites. The hypochondriac is apt to say, "No I am not one to complain, but . . ." The gossip says, "Now I don't mean to say anything about anyone, but . . ." The falsifier prefaces his remarks with "One thing you can always be sure of about me is that I always tell the truth." These efforts are not so much to reassure the listener as to protect the speaker from the implication of what he says, and the prospect of coming face to face with himself.

One of the first steps toward health of personality among such troubled souls is to be able to see and hear themselves as they are. They fool few but themselves. But they do not start down the road to health of spirit until they are able to stop fooling themselves. Worship gives us a chance to stand off and look at ourselves as if we were somebody else, for only then can we see ourselves as we are. It helps us to interpret our behavior and our attitudes as they are. It helps us to take stock of our progress on life's journey without stopping the journey or damaging ourselves.

Worship stimulates faith. It creates the mood where strong belief can be practiced. It generates the atmosphere for creative spiritual activity that can restore sanity and guarantee healthful attitudes toward life and its problems.

This is not to say that those whose sanity is in doubt need only to be taken to a service of worship for restoration. But it is to say that the regular and effective involvement of mind and spirit in the disciplines and arts of worship will prevent many of the states of mind that lead to unbearable stress and breakdown.

For it is at this point that worship traditionally has been its own justification. It has been able to bring together in a healing relationship the conscious and preconscious communications that man has devised to relate his lonely and imprisoned self to those about him and to that beyond him which can give meaning and purpose to the struggles of existence.

Wherever you go, you will find the variations of tradition and national interest and cultural concommitants, but you will also find a common struggle to bring worth to life. Wherever the voice of a pastor is lifted before his flock, there too is the act of seeking worthship for life. For the common mystic cord binding together all branches of the Church and all periods of history is that central effort to give significance to life by relating it to its Creator. Some churches have emphasized ritual, others the prophet's voice, others music, while still others have valued silence, but in each, and always, the act of worship is the common bond satisfying basic human needs.

For our purpose, it is important to try to know how the act of worship produces the conditions that are beneficial to the personality, and how the act of preaching can co-operate with these factors rather than counteract them. Perhaps a clue is found in the statement of a group psycho-therapist working in this field. "In whatever motive power the arts may reside—a product of the unconscious, a suppressed sexuality, or an attempt to counteract the fear of nature's mysterious forces—they inspire, socialize and educate."[2]

Life is continually in need of being lifted up. The word *inspire* implies an endowment of spirit. A church steeple is often referred to as a spire. The arts of worship can furnish this inspiration. It is the role of the arts to mediate inspiration in uncontaminated form. The inspiration that is coupled with a denial of reality seeks to sustain the soul with food that is false. The inspiration that comes through the arts speaks more directly to the unconscious levels of being and is not so apt to be misunderstood. The consciousness of the person combined with his unconscious responses takes what he needs and is not confounded by what may injure his sense of balance or reality.

When in the mood of worship one hears the words of scripture read, he cannot easily separate himself from the great ideas contained in them nor from the great tradition that has been nourished on them. The words take on a meaning that speaks to him of faith and hope, and the significance of his own life is bound up with the lives of others who have heard and responded to such traditional words. The power of holy writ to deal with life and its problems has been attested to in numerous therapeutic relationships. The artful poetry of the Psalms, with their rhythms of thought and phrase, moves the problem of the individual beyond the individual, both as to its existence and the resources for meeting it. Once that is done the problem becomes one of a lesser degree and is more effectively faced.

In his religious architecture, man has always tried to bring inspiration to his spirit through an art form. The temples, the churches, the cathedrals are designed to create a response, emotional and spiritual, that draws up from within the individual some innate need and capacity to reach upward. Who can deny the response of the "organism as a whole" when he walks into a Gothic cathedral with its lofty arches, its rich color and its mood of ageless and vibrant stillness? There is the atmosphere of inspiration. Whether there is a service of worship or not, there is the mood of worship. Man is inspired by what he and his co-seekers have made in their effort to communicate their capacity for spiritual fulfillment. He hears, he feels, he sees, and the communication is real for him.

Man is a social being, but his socialization is never an easy or uncomplicated compromise. His individualism is always compromised at a price. The demands of civilization are continually placing a stress on his capacity for compromise. There is continual need for those forces that can ease the demands of his socialization. The arts employed in religious activity serve such a purpose, for they glorify the aloneness and the togetherness of man at the same time and in so doing minimize the persistent conflict of the self and that which would limit the self.

"The arts have always served as a medium for bringing people together and uniting them. And of them all, there is no equal to music as a cementing force, a force which at once creates unity and intimacy, even in the most heterogeneous congregation. . . . Racial and lingual barriers, differences in creed or education, are easily surmounted by the musical message."[3] Thus a psychiatrist evaluates the socializing function of music.

When a congregation participates in musical response, they are united at several levels. First the music of the bells calls them to come apart from the community and become one in the act of worship. Once within the church the music of the organ pulls down around them a wall of melody and rhythm, religious in content and connotation, that does two things. First, it continues the process of separation from the outer and distracting forces of life, and second, it unites the congregation in a common effort to seek and to find those values that may make them one. The singing of the choirs creates a unity of response as word and melodic line join to stimulate an emotional and intellectual response.

Perhaps most significant of all is the use of congregational singing. Here in poetic form, and with simple and dignified melodic line, the basic beliefs of the faith are sung. These ideas are made so simple and direct that persons accept them without contemplation or evaluation. With an approach to the subconscious that is direct and immediate, the hymns make the creed implicit and explicit at one and the same time. Because the creed is presented informally it is subject to modification without penalty for heresy. So the early Puritans in long hymns that were almost epic poems sang of punishment for the pleasures they were denied but which they were enjoying vicariously through their group singing. So also the followers of a Prince of Peace can lift their voices in battle hymns so stirring that they are able to fulfill the more bellicose emotional and social needs of the singers.

Perhaps someone should make a careful study of the emotional satisfactions that lie hidden deep within the practice of hymn singing. Certainly the role of the emotions cannot be overlooked when a group of adolescents or bachelor ladies sing with feeling, "I come to the garden alone, . . . and he walks with me and he talks with me and he tells me I am his own."

When the frustrations of life become acute, strength is found in singing together such a hymn as John Bunyan's "He who would valiant be 'gainst all disaster" or "God is my strong salvation, what foe have I to fear."

Thus group responses are strengthened when personal satisfactions can only be approximated. At such times the group becomes more truly one, both consciously and, more significantly, unconsciously. This force is so strong that it is employed in times of national crisis to give community spirit, and in war to give heightened morale to fighting men.

However examined, there runs through the traditional music of the church, the qualities of identity, unity, and community. Few religious groups have been able to function without the aid of music. Those that have found the strongest group response have invariably been those whose musical expressiveness was most direct and appealing. The power of music to exert a strong influence within the group is unquestioned. That it may often be beneficial is not denied but is verified scientifically.

The educational function of the arts has long been practiced. The early Hebrews taught through poetry and music. The graphic arts have long exerted a direct appeal to the mind as well as to the other levels of consciousness that make up the total response of the individual. In fact, the inventive capacity of the artist has often exerted a significant uplifting effect upon the group. Many of the insights developed by the theoretical and the applied scientist were first employed by the novelist or the poet. The scientists of personality have gained important insights from such novelists, dramatists and poets as Marlowe, Goethe and Shakespeare. Even the imagination of the aviator and navigator could not have been unaware of the Magic Carpet and Jules Verne.

The use of the mural and the mosaic in the place of worship has also had its direct impact on the individual and collective mind of the worshipper. In services where the language spoken was archaic and unfamiliar, the languages of the arts continued to speak directly and forcefully. Those who speak now to groups cannot be unaware of the influence of the graphic, rhythmic and verbal arts upon the minds of those who listen. These ancillary factors involved in worship are probably more important in creating the setting for the response to preaching than is realized.

If these art forms are able to stimulate a direct response that inspires, socializes and educates, it would seem important for the spoken word to supplement rather than deny the elements within which it is set. The inspiration of the arts, for instance, is direct and relatively uncomplicated. It can supplement the expression of faith, but it does not as easily supplement a denial of reality, for the lower levels of consciousness are not concerned over the logical problems of denying or affirming as much as they are over bringing to bear the response of the "organism as a whole." It might seem then that the preacher must be responsive to the surroundings of worship. While he would inspire he would not couple his inspiration with a denial of reality that violates the function of worship. While he would stimulate courage, he would not seek a foolhardiness that would deny reason. While he would stimulate a strong faith, he would not ignore the obligations of man to self and to society.

Tradition places certain limitations and imposes an exacting discipline upon the preacher. He never forgets that his message is part of a service of worship. As he values the function of worship in individual life and the Christian tradition, so he also recognizes his rights and duties as a leader of worship. There is always something incongruous about trivial preaching in a framework of the majestic hymns and the eternal scriptures. If preaching were a political speech or a social club lecture, it would serve a purpose foreign to that of the pulpit. Should the pulpit be made indistinguishable from the soapbox, both would suffer, and freedom of speech and freedom of worship would confuse their goals in too great a consciousness of their common origin.

This primacy of worship is always in the preacher's mind as he enters the pulpit, for he is first of all a custodian of a sacred tradition. The church as a worshipping body comes first. The church makes its preachers, the preachers do not make the church. The worshipping people are the source of the sermon, for in truth their lives and their needs mold and make the preacher. As a doctor examines his patient before reaching for the medicine, so the pastor senses the needs of the worshipping people before he starts to preach. He views them with a consciousness that they are the church, the body of worshippers with whom it is his privilege to share the insights revealed to him in study and meditation.

If we understand the function of worship as a sanity-restoring and health-creating activity of the spirit, we see the place of preaching as a part of it in a different light. Then the words of the preacher are not independent of the service of worship, but are a part of its perspective-giving, appreciation-perceiving and insight-creating discipline of the human spirit.

If we would understand the function of preaching as a healing word spoken to groups, we would seek to understand the effect of the setting within which that word is spoken. While no definitive answer can be made, we have given a few clues that may indicate a direction. Perhaps we are prepared now to examine more carefully the function of preaching as a part of that quest of wholeness which is man's spiritual birthright.

5

GROUP RESPONSE

SCIENTIFIC conclusions about group behavior have arrived at some judgments that may be discouraging to
the preacher. These objective judgments were first stated
many years ago by pioneer students of human behavior and
have varied little with the years. They may be sum-

95

marized by saying that the group response is a primitive type of reaction, and that the reversions observed are generally away from the desired goals of personal competence and emotional maturity.

It has been pointed out that the group seems responsive to whatever encourages a superficial unity at a level which denies reality, or at least a part of it. Some observers feel that truth is an individual standard and that a group does not care about truth.

It was this conclusion about groups that led Freud to make his early judgments against the religious group and also to raise serious questions concerning group psychotherapy. He wrote, "Groups have never thirsted after truth. They demand illusions, and cannot do without them. They constantly give what is unreal precedence over what is real: they are almost as strongly influenced by what is untrue as by what is true. They have an evident tendency not to distinguish between the two."[1]

If we are going to examine honestly what takes place in the religious group, especially in response to the preaching activity of one who is set apart with a certain father status and therefore a certain group authority, we cannot ignore the challenge implicit in Freud's words: "A group is subject to the truly magical power of words; they can evoke the most formidable tempests in the group mind, and are also capable of stilling them."[2]

In recent years we have seen this verified by the actions of the German people in response to Hitler. We hesitate to look at some group religious responses with quite the same candor.

Le Bon, who exerted a strong influence on Freud, wrote in *The Crowd* that "as soon as living beings are gathered together in certain numbers, no matter whether they are a herd of animals or a collection of human beings, they place themselves instinctively under the authority of a chief." Further: "A group is an obedient herd, which could never live without a master. It has such a thirst for obedience that it submits instinctively to anyone who appoints himself its master."[3] However, the implicit pessimism of such a view was modified a bit by Le Bon's admission that in certain circumstances the morals of a group can be higher than those of the individuals that compose it, and that only collectivities are capable of a high degree of unselfishness and devotion.

As Freud looked at the group, he saw a process that heightened emotions and reduced intellectual controls. "His emotions become extraordinarily intensified, while his intellectual ability becomes markedly reduced, both processes being evidently in the direction of the approximation of the other individuals in the group."[4]

Such a response places in the hands of the group leader a considerable power, but it also involves a commensurate responsibility. It has been found that there are simple ways of building a group response and also rather simple ways of returning the group to a number of individuals. While we are not prepared to say what is desired or desirable, we are able to say with increasing understanding that the leader needs to know what he is doing before he promiscuously creates or destroys something that is valuable to the group.

Those who have spent much time speaking to groups

know of those moments when the group seems to be delivered into their hands, and the emotional response is so intense that they are able to exert a compelling power. The speaker is equally aware of the times when nothing seems able to move the group from its stolid preoccupations with the attitudes that limit its response.

Perhaps it is the distinction between the physical group and the psychological group that makes the difference. Le Bon says at this point, "The most striking peculiarity presented by a psychological group is the following. Whoever be the individuals that compose it, however like or unlike be their mode of life, their occupations, their character, or their intelligence, the fact that they have been transformed into a group puts them in possession of a sort of collective mind which makes them feel, think, and act in a manner quite different from that in which each individual of them would feel, think and act were he in a state of isolation. There are certain ideas and feelings which do not come into being, or do not transform themselves into acts except in a provisional being formed of heterogeneous elements, which for a moment are combined, exactly as the cells which constitute a living body form by their reunion a new being from those possessed by each of the cells singularly."[5]

It seems that something working at a submerged level of consciousness may be operative to explain the change between the individual and the individual in the group. Speaking as if this state might be comparable to hypnosis, Le Bon says further, "Such also is approximately the state of the individual forming part of a psychological group.

He is no longer conscious of his acts. In his case, as in the case of the hypnotized subject, at the same time that certain faculties are destroyed, others may be brought to a high degree of exaltation. Under the influence of a suggestion, he will undertake the accomplishment of certain acts with irresistible impetuosity. This impetuosity is the more irresistible in the case of groups than in that of the hypnotized subject, from the fact that, the suggestion being the same for all the individuals of the group, it gains in strength of reciprocity."[6]

This feeling of reciprocity may be very great in the religious group where the response to the leader is intensified by a common devotion to that for which the leader speaks. Some of what we see in revival meetings as well as the reactions of the group and members within the group to mass healing activities may be described in Le Bon's further evaluation. "We see, then, that the disappearance of the conscious personality, the predominance of the unconscious personality, the turning by means of suggestion and contagion of feelings and ideas in an identical direction, the tendency to transform the suggested ideas into acts; these, we see, are the principal characteristics of the individual forming part of a group. He is no longer himself, but has become an automaton who has ceased to be guided by his will." If that is the case it is clearly seen how important becomes the moral responsibility of anyone who seeks to substitute his will for that of the will vacated under the pressure of group response.

Bishop Matthew Simpson who was famous a century ago had a power over groups that at times embarrassed him. When he felt spiritually led he was able to exert a compelling influence over his hearers just as if he had achieved a state of mass hypnosis. It is recorded that one Sunday morning he brought the congregation at a Methodist Conference so completely under his influence that they wandered off about town aimlessly for hours much to the consternation of the women of the Church, who had fried hundreds of chickens for what they had reason to believe might be a hungry congregation. Bishop Simpson evidently possessed a gift for exerting a strong group suggestion that was intensified by forces within the group itself until it was so formidable a fact that the good Bishop was puzzled by what he had done.

The religious group, with its traditions, its basic ideas, and its mood-creating activities has already many of the characteristics of the psychological group. As Freud puts it, "Before the members of a random crowd of people can constitute something in the nature of a group in the psychological sense of the word, a condition has to be fulfilled; these individuals must have something in common with one another, a common interest in an object, a similar emotional bias in some situation or other, and some degree of reciprocal influence. The higher the degree of this mental homogeneity, the more readily do the individuals form a psychological group, and the more striking are the manifestations of a group mind." The nature of the worshipping group fulfills the essential qualities of the psychological group and with it must accept the limitations.

With these limitations in mind, Freud pessimistically comes to the conclusion that, "it looks as though the work of Group Psychology was bound to come to an ineffectual end, but it is easy to find a more hopeful escape from the dilemma." His efforts to escape the dilemma were not as hopeful as some of those who followed after him. Freud's evaluation of the group was in most instances bound to a partial and faulty background, religiously and anthropologically. His successors with more accurate information to build on have been spared the dejection of some of his conclusions.

Perhaps the degrading elements of the group are more dramatic than the positive elements. Freud's persistent effort to relate group responses to individual emotional states is nowhere more clearly noted than in his study of panic. "Panic arises either owing to an increase of the common danger or owing to the disappearance of the emotional ties which hold the group together, and the latter case is analagous to neurotic dread."[7]

It is his judgment that the characteristics of panic "are that none of the orders given by superiors are any longer listened to, and that each individual is only solicitous on his own account, and without any consideration for the rest." Thereupon, "the mutual ties have ceased to exist and a gigantic and senseless dread is set free."[8] The presence of panic, however, is the factor that changes a group from a creative functioning unity into an incoherent and destructive group of individuals. It was this quality that impressed McDougall with the collective power of induced and transmitted terror.

McDougall says, "Such a group is excessively emotional, impulsive, violent, fickle, inconsistent, irresolute and extreme in action, displaying only the coarse emotions and the less refined sentiments; extremely suggestible, careless in deliberation, hasty in judgment, incapable of any but the simpler and imperfect forms of reasoning; easily swayed and led, lacking in self-consciousness, devoid of self-respect and of sense of responsibility, and apt to be carried away by the consciousness of its own force, so that it tends to produce all the manifestations we have learnt to expect of any irresponsible and absolute power. . . . Hence its behavior is like that of an unruly child or an untutored passionate savage in a strange situate, rather than like that of a wild beast, rather than like that of human beings."[9]

As if that were the final and determining characteristic of group participation, Freud asserts, ". . . By the mere fact that he forms part of an organized group, a man descends several rungs in the ladder of civilization. Isolated, he may be a cultivated individual; in a crowd, he is a barbarian, that is, a creature acting by instinct. He possesses the spontaneity, the violence, the ferocity, and also the enthusiasm of primitive beings. . . . He then dwells especially upon the lowering in intellectual ability which an individual experiences when he becomes merged in a group."

Freud then goes on to characterize a group. "A group is impulsive, changeable and irritable. It is led almost exclusively by the unconscious. The impulses which a group obeys may according to circumstances be generous or cruel, heroic or cowardly, but they are always so imperious that no personal interest, not even that of self preservation, can make itself felt. Nothing about it is premeditated. Though it may desire things passionately, this is never for long, for it is incapable of perseverance. It cannot tolerate any delay between its desire and the fulfillment of its desires. It has a sense of omnipotence, the notion of impossibility disappears for the individual in a group."[10]

These judgments of the group show little understanding of the importance and the power of the group in transmitting the essentials of personality, culture and individuality. It seems to assume that in some fashion the individual can come full blown into possession of those special qualities that are enjoyed only by the individual. This unreasonable suspicion of the group and unwarranted assumption about the individual are at the base of many of the adverse judgments concerning the religious group.

Pursuing his theses concerning Group Psychology—that the individual inevitably loses his freedom in a group and usually gets something less desirable in return—Freud gives his idea of the religious institution in these terms: "In a church (and we may with advantage take the Catholic Church as a type), as well as in the army . . . the same illusion holds good of there being a head—in the Catholic Church Christ, in the army, the Commander in Chief— who loves all the individuals in the group with an equal love. Everything depends on this illusion; if it were to be dropped, then both Church and army would dissolve, so far as the external force permitted them to. This equal love was expressly enunciated by Christ: 'inasmuch as ye have done it unto one of the least of these, my brethren, ye have done it unto me.' He stands for the individual members of the group of believers in the relation of a kind of elder brother; he is their father-surrogate. All demands that are made on the individual are derived from this love of Christ's. A democratic character runs through the Church, for the very reason that before Christ everyone is equal, and that everyone has an equal share in his love. It is not without a deep reason that the similarity between the Christian community and the family is involved, and that believers call themselves brothers in Christ, that is, brothers through the love which Christ has for them. There is no doubt that the tie which unites each individual with Christ is also the cause of the tie which unites them with one another."[11]

It is with this same characteristic in mind that Freud asserts that "all the members must be equal to one another, but they all want to be ruled by one person. . . . Let us venture, then, to correct Trotter's pronouncement that man is a herd animal and assert that he is rather a horde animal, an individual creature in a horde led by a chief." To support this thesis, Freud details the methods used historically by groups who sought ways of raising up and deifying a leader. Unfortunately, Freud had no close working relationship with a democratic society or a free church.

Also Freud was bound to a rather cramped view of science and its insight. Addicted to 19th century scientism, he thought that only science was free of illusion. Would that we might have a chance to get his reaction to what 20th century physical science has done to the illusions that so characterized the 19th century physics! For one who did so much to free the emotions and its response to intuitive judgment, it seems incongruous for him to write that

104

". . . the problem of the nature of the world, irrespective of our perceptual mental apparatus, is an empty abstraction without practical interest." Or further: "No, science is no illusion. But it would be an illusion to suppose that we could get anywhere else what it cannot give us."[12]

So the faulty judgments, applied to the areas of science, seem also to have been applied to the observation of group response. Because his frame of reference was too restricted, he found that which supported his desired ends rather than the facts of the case. He vehemently desired to free individuals from that which bound them, and in his desire to do so, he overlooked an area of human experience that inseparably bound the individual to the group, for good or ill. It remained for those who came after him to gain a more balanced picture of the group response. To him goes credit for presenting with clarity and forcefulness the "ill." To others lies the task of seeing more clearly the "good."

Later writers in the field have done away with the myth of purely scientific practice in these fields. Atkin, writing in the quarterly *American Journal of Psychotherapy* says, "One observes adherents to the three main schools,— Freudian, Jungian and Adlerian,—working in full faith, eliciting differing psychodynamic explanations from similar types of cases, obtaining not very different percentages of cures. Further, one notes that even in any one particular school a strictly determined scientific technique is far from having been established, so that no two analysts are really doing the same thing."[13]

With a high regard for scientific method and observation,

McDougall takes a long look at what takes place in a group and makes constructive suggestions as to how the group can be protected from its weaker aspects, and strengthened. He says, "The collective lowering of intellectual ability is avoided by withdrawing the performance of intellectual tasks from the group and reserving them for individual members of the group."[14]

It is this method that is employed by raising questions which can only be answered in individual terms. Here the work of the intellect must be directed by individuals though at the same time they may be supported by the group atmosphere and the induced group responses. This was the method used in preaching and speaking by Jesus, and is also essentially the method that is used in the analytic group approach.

McDougall goes further to indicate five conditions for raising the collective mental life to a higher level. First, he feels it is important to have some degree of continuity in the existence of the group. This would tend to be the case with most parish congregations. Second, it is necessary to create in each individual member some definite concept of the nature, compcsition, functions, and capacities of the group, so that from this the individual may develop an emotional relation to the group as a whole. Certainly the worshipping group has this. Third, McDougall feels it is important to have some creative interaction or rivalry with other comparable groups that differ in notable respects. Here, at last, is some justification for denominationalism. Fourth, he emphasizes the importance of group customs, traditions and habits that help establish the relations of one member of the group with another. How often a group reacts negatively to a change in the order of worship. Fifth, the group should have some definite structure, expressed in the specialization and differentiation of the function of its constituents. So the choirs, ushers, and participants play varied roles but together they create the structure that helps to preserve the individual while the group function is enhanced.

McDougall, though willing to face the limitations on much of group life, is not bound by them, and sees the possibilities for the contribution of the creative group response to the lives of the members of the group. And significantly enough the ways he suggests for lifting the level of group life are not different from those employed regularly in the religious group.

But the most desirable condition for the life of the religious group is that which approximates the healthy, normal life of the family, where there is growth, and learning and realistic evaluation in an atmosphere of acceptance. The home is seldom a place of artificial inspiration. Rather it is a place of complete honesty and candor, where people are not afraid to be themselves because they know they are willingly accepted as they are.

Slavson in *Creative Group Education* outlines the characteristics shared by the good family and the creative group. "The four major contributions of the good family, and of all group education are: (1) to establish satisfying affective (love) relations with children and with adults; (2) to provide ego satisfactions; (3) to give expression to the creative-dynamic drives of the individual; and, (4) to engender emotions and to establish attitudes that dispose the individual to social usefulness and group participation. These are at once the objectives and the criteria of evaluating good group work." He divides the groups into three general categories, the compulsory group, such as the public school, the motivated group such as the church, and the voluntary group such as social and political clubs.[15]

The motivated group perhaps shares most easily the essential qualifications of the family framework. This motivated group has the basis for structure that can give direction to the dynamic quality of growing life, without destroying it. Here Slavson points out the dangers of the compulsory group. "Recent discoveries reveal man as an electro-chemical mechanism. These discoveries, which may in time revolutionize psychology, medicine, and the social sciences, indicate that the human body is a potential-generating mechanism seeking discharge through some form of physical, intellectual or emotional activity. The nature of such discharge-activity may vary with individuals, but the drive to be active and to create is basic to man's constitution. This activity is a requirement for establishing the inner balance that is necessary to equanimity and tranquillity. Contrary to these principles, formal training and official education are designed to exert restraint." Without accepting all that may be implied by the term *mechanism,* one can recognize the dynamic quality of man's spiritual nature seeking expression, and be aware of the importance of the creative religious group for that purpose.

As quoted elsewhere in this book, Martin Grotjahn, M. D., makes explicit his judgment that the religious group stands alone as a proponent of love and cooperation, and does not need to resort to the lower form of impulse to sustain itself. But if that is the case, there is little justification for it to employ those methods of group activity that might even impede normal growth.

It was at this point that Freud sensed a danger in the religious group. "Man cannot remain a child for ever; he must venture at last into the hostile world. This may be called 'education to reality'; need I tell you that it is the sole aim of my book to draw attention to the necessity for this advance?"

A follower of Freud a generation later makes more explicit the dangers that exist in employing the mood of inspiration to the exclusion of honest facing of one's self. "The group analyst who is psychoanalytically oriented cannot encourage an inspirational atmosphere which represses unconscious factors and creates unstable illusions of success which are bound to be shortlived. He promotes a spirit of deep, mutual examination and review of personal inadequacies and weaknesses. Such a procedure does not destroy the patient but merely attacks his neurotic character structure. Then he draws new strength from the group and rises to higher strata of personal and social coordination which makes unlikely a turning back to old and outmoded forms."[16]

If those working with small groups recognize the danger of the persistent employment of repressive-inspirational techniques to normal emotional and spiritual growth, how much more should those who work with religious groups be aware of these dangers? If those working with such groups recognize the values of the clearly analytical approach in sustaining healthy growth, should not the religiously oriented group be equally discerning?

While an optimistic, faith-oriented approach may be used, and simplicity, honesty, and straightforwardness employed, too much dependency upon the authoritarian leader makes for governing and not growth, restraint and not liberation, inhibition of the emotions rather than their healthy expression. Here the leader has a double responsibility, for he sets the mood and then works to project it.

Slavson says that the characteristics essential for successful group leadership are "Psychological insight, a socialized personality, intellectual hospitality, respect for the personality and views of others, broad social interests and an evolved social philosophy, the capacity to allow others to grow intellectually at their own pace, emotional maturity, cooperativeness, resourcefulness, creativity and respect for the creativity of others, love for people, cheerfulness and evenness of temper, knowledge and humor."[17]

If those who seek to lead the religious group would stand humbly before such a list of qualifications it might add another dimension to their ordination.

We have in this chapter tried to face some of the early criticisms directed at the group, especially as it might be identified with its religious use. We have seen how some of the more recent thinkers have been less pessimistic, although they have laid down some rather sharp limitations for group activity that cannot be easily ignored by those who are responsible for leadership of religious groups. We have tried to evaluate in the light of these studies the roles

110

of the preacher as a leader of the religious group with an inclination toward a repressive-inspirational practice as contrasted with an analytical approach. Perhaps now in conclusion we might turn again to Dr. Freud who in a more philosophical mood raises a question about the ability of the religious group to measure up to the ideas of its great spiritual leaders.

Freud concludes, "In its origin, function and relation to sexual love, the *Eros* of the philosopher Plato coincides exactly with the love force, the libido, of psychoanalysis, as has been shown in detail by Nachmansogn and Pfister; and when the apostle Paul, in his famous letter to the Corinthians, prizes love above all else, he certainly understands it in the same 'wider' sense. But this only shows that men do not always take their great teachers seriously, even when they profess most to admire them."[18]

Perhaps now we are ready to turn from the more theoretical aspect of the subject to the more recent studies that have been made, and add an important practical contribution to our understanding of the forces at work in the religious group.

111

6

GROUP DYNAMICS

*T*HERE IS something about preaching that is change-
less, yet ever changing. One does not read long in the
best preaching of every age before realizing that a characteristic of great preaching is an able interpretation of the
timeless in time, the principles of eternal value in the

changing affairs of men, and the nature of God to people who see God in the light of their peculiar needs and mental conditioning.

The preacher is essentially an artist. He uses words to heal and inspire the troubled souls of men. As with any artist he works at a threefold task: that of expressing his own feeling and insight, of using a medium to do that creatively, and ultimately of communicating to others through his medium the feelings and insights that stir him.

As the preacher in each generation is moved by compassion and filled with insight, he uses the medium of the pulpit to reveal and communicate to others. But in order to be effective he must be sensitive to the capacity for response on the part of his hearers, and at the same time he must be alert to the resources of his medium to stimulate thought and generate feelings that can lead to health of mind, body and spirit.

While an artist may intuitively use his medium creatively, he may learn greater effectiveness by study and research. Many great artists have been adventurers in exploring the resources of their medium. They have sought to know more and more of what the medium could do and how it could best do it.

It seems reasonable that the pastor as preacher should be concerned with the basic purpose and effect of his words. He is essentially a healer of souls through the use of words. His is not only the task of understanding the use of words, but the effect they have on the minds of others. With Theocritus he must know, "Not easy 'tis to know another's mind." But because the task is not easy is no excuse for proceeding in the use of a medium in unexamined complacency.

Those who work in the field of soul healing as approached from the science of medicine are willing to recognize the nature of their art. Dr. I. Atkin, a London psychiatrist, says, ". . . psychotherapy remains more an art than a science and just as there are many styles in art, so there are many types of psychotherapy."[1]

Speaking of one who would seek to learn the art from the medical point of view, he adds, "as the years go on, he will come to realize that his successes depend more on his sympathy, tolerance, patience, kindliness, tact, powers of artistic intuition and his increasing understanding of the polar subtleties of human nature, than to some rigid theoretical system that he had at one time fondly embraced."

Any great art, however, has a demanding discipline and rather exacting standards. One seeks to know all he can about his particular medium of expression in order that he may use it most creatively. So it should be with the art of preaching.

For two thousand years men have been preaching in the Christian church. This preaching has been a powerful influence upon life. Often it brought understanding and inspiration to the lives of people. At other times it was a source of chaos and conflict and life-destroying hatred. But there has been something about the nature of preaching that has met a deep human need and it has survived through the years.

Too often it has been an unexamined art. Persons have

practiced it with little regard for established traditions, and with quite limited understanding of what it might be doing to the lives of those who were affected by it. Perhaps that was true because there were few definitive methods for understanding its effects, and few standards for evaluating the medium as it was employed.

Recent years have produced marked progress in the understanding of such matters as group identity, group dynamics, and group therapy. These may well become new tools for helping to give standards and measurements to the art of preaching. Buried in the dry and often seemingly interminable statistics of the research psychologist, there are insights into the needs of people, the power of words and the healing relationship that can be established between pastor and people.

Those who are interested in effective preaching as a form of ministry to soul needs may well study the history and findings of those who have tried a more exacting approach to group needs and group responses. They have not been unaware of the history of religion as it relates to groups.

Dr. J. W. Klapman in a historical survey of group practice writes that ". . . the elements of an effective therapy have been in more or less wide usage as far back as the memory of man can serve him . . . King Saul rallying his troops to defeat the formidable Philistines, Xenophon marching his men back to Greece, Socrates and his pupils in their peripatetic discourses, and many other instances of influence exerted over groups and masses of people attest to the potency of mass suggestion and mass identification directed toward a given and specific end . . . whenever a teacher, a leader, a central person wittingly or unwittingly attempts to influence any group of individuals he or she is, in effect, employing some of the principles of group psychotherapy."

But Dr. Klapman further indicates that these principles were "used without conscious knowledge of their essential nature . . . toward the more general objective of restoring a desired state of intropsychic equilibrium."[2]

Those who would be more than "blind leaders of the blind" must not only know in their own experience the meaning of "life that is abundant," but more, they must know what it is that can communicate that knowledge to others most surely and most effectively.

As is often the case, insights into the human soul and its relations to life come from strange places. Nearly fifty years ago two physicians working at a French hospital for the mentally ill made a discovery that they thought significant. The patients who were too poor to pay for private rooms and were assigned to a large ward in the institution showed improved condition and were more contented and cheerful. Although they were not in a position to evaluate all the factors involved, Doctors Camus and Pogniez expressed their belief that there was a healing factor in the group relationship that was negated by isolation. Probably that insight of theirs was enough to set ajar the door leading into fuller understanding of the importance of group activity for human well-being.

In this country, the pioneer work in the field was done by Dr. J. H. Pratt in Boston. There again a chance factor was at work. Dr. Pratt was not primarily interested in the mental or emotional factor, but because the number of patients suffering from tuberculosis was too large to be hospitalized, he organized clinical classes for lectures on home care and personal hygiene. He soon noted that their understanding of their illness produced a marked change in their attitude and disposition. They not only felt better, but the group relationship with others who were suffering a similar affliction seemed to produce emotional strength. What started out as an emergency time saving method of treatment became the basis of extended practice of what Dr. Pratt called, "thought control."

In 1922 Dr. Pratt published his observations in a book called *The Principles of Class Treatment and Their Application to Various Chronic Diseases*. Therein is described the class procedure that became ritualized in many respects comparable to a religious service. Classes of chronic patients were seated according to their record of improvement. It was good to improve and improvement was rewarded with increased prestige in the class. Testimonies were given by improved patients. The class was interrupted by relaxation exercises that relieved tension and increased the sense of common welfare. Inspirational poetry was read, and it is reported that from 60 to 70% of the class members improved under this type of treatment. The dynamic factors at work can be noted as similar to those of Alcoholics Anonymous and Christian Science.

Between the times that Dr. Pratt started his studies and published his book about them there were others who became interested in the possibility of group activity. In 1919 Dr. Edward Lazell started treatment, by the group method, of a ward full of patients inaccessible to individual therapy.

He gave a series of lectures on the nature and understanding of their own particular type of illness. In 1930 he reported remarkable results. "Silent, dreamy boys suddenly became interested and drank in every word, realizing that here was someone who understood their problems. Ashamed of themselves and suffering from a profound feeling of inferiority, guilt and failure, and afraid to confess to anybody because they considered themselves unique in their mental degradation, they were greatly relieved when told that all mankind had to contend with the same emotions that had broken them down."

Dr. Jacob Moreno, a student of Freud, started in Vienna in 1911, a "spontaneity theatre" in which persons acted out physically the conflicts that disturbed them. By trying first one role and then another they became aware of the nature of contending forces, and more objectively understood their relationship in life to the problems that disturbed them. Not only did this release tension, but by working with others in the process the problem was exteriorized so that it could be seen and interpreted. For nearly fifty years, Dr. Moreno has been developing this technique until now it is employed in many hospitals and clinics. The literature in the field has become considerable. Conflict continues as to the value and effect of the method, but there seems to be a rather general recognition of the power of the dynamic group forces that is brought to bear through psychodrama, sociodrama and related forms of group psychotherapy.

At Kings Park State Hospital outside of New York City, Dr. L. C. Marsh carried on interesting experiments in the group approach during the 1930s. In an article, "Group

Treatment of the Psychoses by the Psychological Equivalent of the Revival," he tells how to bring a happier state of mind to patients by recreating the factors that seemed to stimulate the human spirit in religious revivals. Gathering together as many as five hundred patients at a time in a large room, he sought to create a festive air. Dr. Marsh availed himself of such techniques as "community singing, stunt activities, spelldowns, testimonials of recovered or improved patients, birthday cakes for patients whose birthday it happened to be, appointment of patient committees, monitors, etc."

Through such efforts he sought to involve patients intellectually and emotionally so that they could begin to operate beyond themselves, break down barriers of separation, and live. In his own words, "My interest is an emotional one; I used the crowd psychology to bring their emotional interests into squad formation, to discipline and direct them toward life. The aim is to extrovert all energies at the social level." It has been Dr. Marsh's contention that institutions for the mentally and emotionally disturbed should be considered as schools rather than hospitals, where the patients are "on condition" in the course in civilization, and need special tutoring to learn how to get along with themselves and others.

Other experiments with children who have feeding problems, and adults with mild disturbances such as high blood pressure and hypertension, seem to indicate that the methods of group involvement, limited competition, reward, and prestige are significant factors in changing human behavior into more healthful patterns. Such groups as "Recovery,

Inc." guided by Dr. Abraham Low in Chicago, have shown the value of lectures, book reviews, study groups, house parties, and their own publication *Lost and Found* in helping to remove the stigma of mental or emotional illness, and share the strength of a common return to health.

Dr. S. R. Slavson, of the Jewish Board of Guardians, has done important work with children and adolescents. This work has demonstrated how the power of the group can bring a personality into new relationship with reality. Working with the Commonwealth Fund he published in 1943 *An Introduction to Group Therapy* in which he makes this conclusion: "The most important value of character formation of group experiences is the modification or elimination of egocentricity and psychological insularity."[3]

These experiments in the field of group work have a direct bearing on the work of the pastor as preacher, for they verify the value of the group method both in bringing inspiration and understanding. If the lecture method can help to restore mental health to a group of seriously disturbed individuals, a carefully directed sermon can certainly do much to help persons meet the milder disturbances of life with strength and understanding.

As Dr. Klapman indicates, "there is a breaking point for every individual, a resultant of interplay of all forces brought to bear on the individual." Through a persistent strengthening of the resources and intropsychic balance of the personality, this breaking point can be warded off. It is at this point that the preaching ministry has been and is still making its great contribution. It is persistently helping people to modify or eliminate the soul killing egocentricity and so involve them with others that they cannot become lost in psychological insularity.

The prevalance of preaching and worship is an indication of the need for it and the value of it. Those who most appreciate the value of preaching will be most anxious to avail themselves of any understanding that can make their time-honored art more helpful. Those who most precisely appreciate the needs of people in our day will be the better qualified to meet those needs most effectively.

Dr. John T. McNeill in *A History of the Cure of Souls* says, "A generation that turns from religion is more and more productive of psychopathic personalities and victims of psychoneurosis and psychosis, and is exposed to the dominance of fanatical psychoneurotics who use psychology itself to destroy personality. The leaders of society and of the churches need to measure critically and justly the possibilities and limitations of scientific psychotherapy in meeting the terrific forces that ravage the interior life of modern man. It is not less important to weigh with the same critical judgment the methods traditionally employed by religious guides of souls."[4]

The resources of "scientific psychotherapy" are so taxed that those who work with groups through the church must sense their responsibility both for preventative and healing work among those who are spiritually bruised though not broken. Dr. Klapman might well be speaking of the task of the preacher when he writes, "A certain enormous and unexplored and unexploited area exists for group therapy which has drawn little attention as yet . . . there are those individuals rendered morose and unhappy by the stresses of living for whom treatment will prove just as efficacious as with the more apparent psychoneurotics and the outright psychotics. These persons are the 'normals' or near normals. No suspicion of mental health attaches to them. The serious psychiatrist does not attempt to think in hard and fast categories for he knows mental health is purely a matter of degree and not of kind . . . the line of distinction . . . [appears when they] begin to relinquish the effort to abide by reality . . . Normals who are eccentric, unhappy, and ill adjusted are also in need of therapy. Theirs are the needs of our entire civilization . . . group therapy with these has significance for the whole social structure."

Preaching comes well within the framework of Dr. Klapman's definition of group psychotherapy: "Any non-physical means used to influence an individual's life toward socially useful ends and also such ends as will at the same time afford the individual the optimum in personal efficiency, security and happiness."

In view of the religious belief that there can be no "optimum" in personal efficiency, security and happiness without a sense of cosmic support and purpose to lend a basis for real self-esteem, it seems that the pulpit has the significant word to say at this point. When we further realize that there can be no real regard for others, no "socially useful ends" that make sense without this basis for adequate self-esteem, it seems that the church's significant place as an instrument for group therapy is established. For the three great affirmations concerning self, others, and cosmic security are central in that command of the Master Physician of Souls who said, "Love the lord your God with

123

all your heart, and soul and mind and strength, and your neighbor as yourself."

One would not do justice to the history of preaching were he to ignore the fact that in every age, through an innate sensitivity to human need and personality forces, the church has made use of group dynamics for the purposes of group healing. "Lying deep in the experience and culture of the early Christian communities are the closely related practices of mutual edification and fraternal correction . . . 'Let us then pursue what makes for peace and for mutual upbuilding' (Rom. 14:19). . . . Confess your sins to one another and pray for one another, that you may be healed' (James 5:16)."

From earliest times, membership in the religious community has been accepted as a mutual defense pact against the powers of darkness that can lead to destruction. The purging practice of public confession, because of difficulties of administration and also adverse effect upon certain types of personalities, was early modified. Private confession became a matter of choice and then the accepted practice, and a whole body of literature having to do with spiritual purification and right living came into being. This was for the guidance of the confessor in his own religious living and in his relationship with the confessee. What had been singularly effective in the group life of the early church as a discipline, became less effective as a private confessional, and with the passing of time became, through ignorance and abuse, a different institution.

It was to the abuses of the confessional that Luther in part addressed himself in his Ninety-Five Theses. It was not that he did not value confession, but he believed it should be voluntary and shorn of those abuses that made it little more than a monetary transaction. For himself, he says, "I would let no man take confession away from me, and I would not give it up for all the treasures of the world, since I know what comfort and strength it has given me." The effect of Luther's challenge was to make the concern for the troubled soul more a matter for personal response than a matter of sacramental form. It seems that Luther himself, in pastoral practice, sought to establish what we now call "rapport" with troubled souls in order to lead them to understanding and peace. This of course led to a new constellation of human relationships in groups formed for the purpose of counselling together about the Christian way of life.

It was the prayer group of Moravians that caused Wesley to search his own soul. The Holy Club of Oxford was utilizing group dynamics in a manner that so impressed Wesley he built the Methodist Revival in England around this small group. Never since that time has the small group emphasis been entirely out of the picture. Though the mass revival has had its day, the small group has always been a power. Wesley's works indicate a singular understanding of effective group organization. Bands, so called, of from five to ten members were built around a group loyalty to the faith in practice. Classes composed of a dozen members met once a week under a leader "for mutual edification through testimony, and fellowship in prayer and praise." Wesley felt that the small group was as important as public worship, and the vitality of the Wesleyan movement testifies to the significant use he made of group dynamics.

One cannot easily estimate the far reaching effort of the small group movement as developed by the Quakers on the social thought of our country. Group activity may have a healing effect upon society as well as upon the individual. The Christian Science movement, with its emphasis on denial of illness and its testimony to health is a striking illustration of the repressive-inspirational group technique. The Oxford Group Movement with its emphasis on confession and purgation may illustrate the more introspective and self-analytical approach to group technique. More recently we have seen Alcoholics Anonymous grow rapidly through its application of the repressive-inspirational technique to the problems of the alcoholic.

Such groups, from New Testament times to the present, have employed the mutual aid factor, and have recognized the power that exists within the group to heal souls. They have indicated group dynamics at work in so distinctive a fashion that students of group therapy from the medical and scientific approach have recognized the unique contribution to be made through them.

Dr. Martin Grotjahn, a California psychiatrist, in writing on the *Use of Emotions in Psychotherapy,* indicates the significance of the group organization that is oriented to a principle beyond itself. "It is much easier to activate group emotions of hostile opposition and destruction than of tolerance and cooperation. A group feels strength in hate and in fight. The group feels broken up into weak individuals when love and cooperation is asked. Only the religious group is firm in faith and belief. It is united and, therefore, does not necessarily need hatred as a unifying factor."

If, as this would seem to indicate, there is something unique in the power of a religious group to unite people for creative goals, it is quite obvious that the religious group has a significant role to play in a world with such destructive forces as atomic fission and bacteriological techniques for mass destruction. If preaching is one of the media of group organization and direction, it now enters the time and place of unusual significance in the affairs of men. If, at the same time, there are developed new insights into the use of preaching as a technique for determining group understanding and group response, we have arrived at an important crossroad in history. A great human need challenges us to use new sources of understanding of the dynamics of human behavior.

Because of the regard for human personality, it is impossible to set up carefully regulated experiments with certain types of group behavior. The medical profession would not encourage war in order to study new techniques in surgery, but the exigencies of war forced the medical corps to make radical changes in practice in order to meet human needs. As the First World War had significant effect on the practice of surgery, so the Second World War made a definite contribution to the study of group behavior, group dynamics, and group therapy.

For the first time in history there was the type of organized knowledge and psychological testing technique to evaluate what was taking place among groups of people who were operating under terrific emotional pressures. Here again, this information gained under extreme conditions can be valuable in helping us to understand human behavior under comparable circumstances with milder emotional stimuli.

Dr. Joost A. M. Meerloo, analyst and author, has made important contributions to the understanding of panic, suffering, sorrow, and the psychology of war through his observations of human behavior in Amsterdam under German bombing and occupation. After Dr. Meerloo escaped to England he was able to observe the behavior of English people under war conditions. Thus, through seeing how individuals behaved under the stimulus of fear, he was able to formulate insights into behavior that correlate knowledge of physiology, psychology, and psychiatry. Such insights can be useful in defining the dynamics of fear so that when we preach to the fearful in times of stress we will with intelligent purpose use resources that can be effective.[4]

Dr. Meerloo classified the fear reaction in group form or panic into four types. Regression involves the reversion to a more primitive type of behavior where adults act like children and forget their learning. Camouflage is characterized by a loss of identity and an effort to assume the nature of the surroundings even though this may cause denial of moral and cultural identities. Motor-explosion is the adult equivalent of the temper tantrum in whatever form it may express itself. Conversion involves an interiorization of stress with a variety of immediate or delayed psychosomatic disturbances. In order to know better the scientific resources for understanding human emotion, let us look more closely at each of these classifications of fear reaction.

One of the defenses that the human organism uses against fear is a type of regression to more primitive forms of existence. This can be seen at the biological level by a bodily regression in response to a cut or injury. Immediately the body builds a temporary fibrous tissue of a primitive type of structure before proceeding to replace the injured tissue with the more highly developed and differentiated type. This is all well and good unless the regressed and primitive tissue gets out of control and follows its own rules and not the body's higher needs. This is what happens in the case of malignant tissue, for the cancer cell is a primitive type that does not serve the body.

What is true biologically is also true emotionally or psychologically. Under the pressure of extreme danger, the behavior pattern regresses and the learned controls deteriorate. Patterns of toilet training are forgotten in temporarily or chronically frightened children. Primitive types of behavior such as "freezing" or flight may make rational or normal adult behavior difficult or impossible. Soldiers under stress may cower and cringe like frightened animals or they may fight and destroy with a frenzied abandon that also shows the snarling disregard for pain and danger of an attacking animal, but in both instances the reaction is regressed and fear-stimulated.

The same quality of regression may show in group behavior patterns. The frightened mob in panic reverts to a collective herd pattern of action. When galvanized into action by strong fright stimuli it may operate with reckless abandon toward individual members of the group, thus operating not as a group of individuals with reason, but as a new entity without reason and at a primitive level of emotion. Under the pressure of what amounts to group hypnosis, persons can be led to revert to childish types of behavior where they ritualize their fears, come to believe in magic, make strange and unreasonable expressions of faith, and accept the fantastic rather than the reasonable. The history of religion is replete with illustrations of this type of mass action which denies, in action, the elements of mature religion, and reverts to the pattern of childish belief and behavior.

Camouflage also shows its effect at different levels. We know how lower forms of life like the snow rabbit, the ermine, and the chameleon change their colors in response to the need for protection against natural enemies they fear. We are less inclined to think that humans react in such a manner. However it is a commonplace fact that hair can turn white from fear, and I have seen large blotches on the skin that occurred during fright and remained permanently. We know of the more common skin reactions such as goose pimples and hair standing on end that are the result of fear. These are all primitive physiological responses to fear that are related to an effort to change appearance when endangered.

The individual also develops psychological defense mechanisms to make him harmonize with his surroundings. The criminal will lose himself in a crowd. The person with unpopular attitudes and feelings will do things consciously or unconsciously to lose his identity in relation to those whom he fears. He may lose his identity completely and become amnesic. Or he may partly lose his identity by a process of forgetting. Or he may in varying degrees adopt an attitude of fantasy where he denies the reality of his surroundings by making other mental environs for himself. He may use words and actions to cover up his feelings rather than express them and, in inhibition or repression, become temporarily a different person. To a greater or lesser degree this is common practice. The sensitive person is suspicious of others. The person who is afraid of being talked about becomes the gossip.

This same use of camouflage on the group level is seen when a mob uses hatred and violence to protect itself against an imagined challenge to its superiority. The psychic quality of the frightened mob is something different from the sum-total psychic quality of the individuals that make it up. The group compulsions in Hitler Germany could lead the crowd to deny what the individuals affirmed because of the fears of reprisal and the distrust in the civil liberties granted the individual. The suspicion, insecurity, and fear which the individual might normally contend against, were lost in the crowd impulse to seek a collective safety from what threatened all. The individual is persistently threatened by isolation and separation, and in the group framework he will deny his individuality and rationality to find the protection of the group mind which is ready and willing to adapt itself to the conditions threatening its security.

Fear also shows itself through such adult equivalents of the temper tantrum as fight and uncoordinated flight. Physiologically the organism reacts with a spasm of activity. Every muscle is brought into play whether needed or not. The physical action may be so disorganized that only a slight tremor affects the body, or the body action may be so coördinated that the result is sudden, rapid and surprising flight. The physical organism gives way to emotional pressures and they in turn evoke muscular expression that is beyond the power of the reason or the control mechanisms to restrain.

The psychological factor involved at the individual level is easily identified. It is the accumulation of emotional pressures that have been restrained with difficulty until the breaking point is reached. In primitive tribes such behavior has been observed following severe earthquakes which disrupt the basic faith of the individual in the earth itself. Overcome with fear, the individual "runs amuck" and gives unbridled expression to his now released emotions. In the case of the New Jersey veteran who "ran amuck" and killed several relatives and others who got in his way, the same psychological mechanism was probably at work.

At the group level this thing can be seen in such behavior as that of the Italian soldiers at Caporato who broke under the stress of persistent pressure, lost all sense of discipline, and in panic killed each other and any civilians who were around. The mass reaction to the realistic radio presentation by Orson Welles of an H. G. Wells play about an invasion of Martians was the uncontrolled emotional reaction of insecure people. In occupied Germany and in postwar Japan similar incidents have occurred repeatedly. The tantrum as an uncontrolled response to factors that are too great to handle with reason can be a group phenomenon as well, especially in a differentiated and interdependent society where everyone lives in a rather precarious security.

Perhaps most general and most serious because of its varied and delayed forms of reaction to fear and anxiety is the phenomenon of conversion, using the term psychologically. The physiological phenomena here are rather easily noted. The fear response is internalized and may show itself through contractions of the blood vessels that increase heart strain and eventually cause heart failure. Or it may show in high blood pressure, colitis, stomach disturbance, frequent urination, and similar psychogenic symptoms. The personality keeps itself under a firm control emotionally, but at such an effort that the internal mechanism is seriously disturbed in the process.

Psychologically this same fear shows itself through behavior that seeks to protect the emotions from injury. A child who has been emotionally injured through unfortunate child-parent relations may proceed with great caution in establishing other significant human relations. He may resist expressions of affection, and show that he does not trust love. A child has limited knowledge of the outside world and its dangers, but he has a great consciousness of inner danger. Similarly, an adult who has been emotionally injured may change or condition the normal types of emotional response until his inner defenses protect him from what he feels is threatening. It is readily seen how emotional conversions of this type can have a marked effect on the marriage relationship.

133

In a group response the same conversion factors may be at work. A nation may be so conditioned that it will seek to ignore or deny those characteristics that indicate tenderness or goodwill. Organized around fantasies of injustice and prejudice, such as the Versailles Treaty and anti-Semitism, a nation of people may change their basic traits from scientific understanding and advanced social thinking to pseudo-science and a modified medievalism. In the process the group learns, almost automatically, to respond in childish fashion to symbols, images, words and mass behavior that are closely related to childish patterns of thought. In effect the adult group trades in its maturity for the security it finds in subjection to a dictator or parent figure who meets the fantasy needs of internalized fears.

One cannot study with care the formalized observations of the study of individuals and groups under stress of fear and anxiety without growing in understanding of the factors that affect normal people in modern society to a greater or lesser degree. Such insight inevitably becomes a factor to condition the purpose and the content of the group experience involved in public worship and preaching.

Drs. Adorno, Levinson et al., have completed the first of a series of studies that reveal not only the characteristics of the emotions of the congregation under stress, but indicate something of the type of response that is to be expected from a certain type of pulpit figure. We have all seen the authoritarian preacher who speaks with the "Thus Saith the Lord" approach. But seldom have we been able to understand what was involved in the type of control exerted by that approach. In *The Authoritarian Personality*, a study by

Drs. Adorno and Levinson, we see taking form the personality needs that look for such controls on the one hand and the personality needs that seek to exert such controls on the other. We cannot escape the implications of such studies for the understanding of the preaching function, for the preacher's understanding of his own personality needs will help him to understand his obligation to the group, just as an understanding of the needs of the group will make it possible for him to better understand his power and his limitations in dealing with people.[5]

Such studies of anxiety as those published recently by Rollo May and Drs. Hoch and Zubin pave the way for a deeper understanding of the relation between fear and its disorganizing counterpart in anxiety. Increasingly the tools are being forged for the conscientious preacher who is genuinely concerned about what he is and should be doing with people. Ways are becoming available to analyse his art and use his medium with greater precision than has ever been possible before.

The scientific study of what takes place in group therapy, plus the basic studies in the area of group emotions and group dynamics, make it possible to build on that genius of history revealed through the ages by sensitive preachers. Thus a new and higher level of healing efficiency can be gained for those who would preach the healing Word.

7

WHERE DISCIPLINES MEET

*T*HE KIND of preaching that sees people, that makes them feel they are loved because they are understood, invites an active personal response on the part of the listener. The kind of preaching that encourages maturity, that makes people want to solve their problems by growth in self-understanding, leads to growing pains of the spirit that stimulate personal counseling. The kind of preaching that seeks to release the resources of love in each individual, will bring those who suffer from a log-jam of the emotions to someone who can help them to sort out their feelings and thus direct their natural inclinations toward their worthy goals.

When a preacher employs an understanding approach to his people, he can expect that they will seek him out for further aid in the complicated task of living. They will say to themselves, "There is one who understands me. I can go to him for help and not condemnation." For person-conscious preaching inevitably leads to a response on the part of those who are conscious of personal problems. Woe to the preacher who creates the mood for that sort of reaction and then is unprepared or unable to meet it.

What is pastoral counseling? Rollo May, who is one of the more dependable guides in the techniques of counseling, says it is "any deep understanding between persons which results in the changing of personality." The pastor's specific function is, of course, to encourage changes in personality toward a more mature, resourceful, and loving personality.

Of all those groups of persons who are concerned with the personality problems of individuals, the Christian pastor is in a unique position. His concept of the mind and its function is neither mechanistic nor materialistic. He may accept the import of theories of the unconscious and sub-conscious, and use those insights for his larger purposes, but basically he has a faith in a supraconscious capacity within the mind and soul of each creature, and with all of his scientific understanding he does not overlook that which is beyond science—or at least not included in the present scope of scientific interpretation.

In his efforts to save men from what Pitrim Sorokin calls "the dominant Sensate Culture," he may use the tools developed within that culture for a purpose well beyond the capacity of that culture to appreciate. Students of counseling whose training and orientation have been dominated by the mechanistic or materialistic view of personality, may easily lose sight of their chief goal as Christian pastors. The mechanistic and materialistic view of personality tries to interpret the spirit by the biological mind, while the Christian view of personality seeks to understand mind in its relation to its spiritual counterpart in the cosmos, and gives it cosmic significance, purpose and meaning. As Sorokin would express it, "The biological unconscious lies below the level of the conscious energies and the supraconscious (genius, creative élan, the extrasensory, the divine inspiration, supraconscious intuition, etc.) lies above the level of any conscious, rational and logical thought or energy."

Certainly, when the intellectual stirrings of many of the more daring minds of our generation are reaching toward some form of spiritual integration is no time for the custodians of a Christian concept of personality to approach their function with an attitude that denies their trust. Sorokin speaks of the "idealistic," Nicolas Berdyaev projects a "New Medieval" with its spiritual emphasis; Otto Spengler outlines the culture of a "New Religiosity," and Arnold Toynbee speaks of a "New Universal Church." Dr. Von

Domarus, psychiatrist and teacher, indicates that the whole sweep of anthropology is toward the highest conceivable level of life, "the religious man." No theory of man and life that tried to solve personality problems on a materialistic level of performance would be satisfactory to the pastor in his counseling approach.

As Dr. Sorokin points out, we are involved in a period of changing emphasis in the concept of human personality. There is a transition "from predominantly materialistic, egoistic, hedonistic, utilitarian, mechanistic, and cerebrally-rational to predominantly idealistic, spiritual, altruistic, organic and supraconscious or intuitional" ideas of the human soul, society and culture.

The most personal of relations into which the pastor enters, that of personal counseling, must not be allowed to run counter to the important philosophical and theoretical advances of our day. And there is no need that it should, for the tools of science can be used without a necessary adherence to the theoretical limitations of that science. The hammer and the saw may be used to build a hot-dog stand or a chapel. It is the design of the builder that determines the employment of the tools. So the tools of psychological insight may justify a sinner or discipline a saint, for it is the design of the builder of personality that determines the employment of the tools.

No less an authority than Dr. Carl Jung indicates that "in its development up to the present, psychology has dealt chiefly with psychic processes in the light of physical causation, [but] the future task of psychology will be the investigation of their spiritual determinants . . . Psychological research has not as yet drawn aside all the many veils from the picture of the human psyche; it remains as unapproachable and obscure as all the deep secrets of life." Yet he is explicit on the point of his own practice as a psychiatrist, for he says, "If I recognize only naturalistic values, and explain everything in physical terms, I shall depreciate, hinder, or even destroy the spiritual development of my patients."

The pastor's chief interest is the spiritual development of his people. How can he best combine his function as a teacher of spiritual truth and as a pastoral counselor with his new obligations to the insights of psychological science? The answer probably lies in a carefully understood and practiced synthesis of the two disciplines of mind and spirit.

Yet for the average pastor this synthesis may not come easily. How can he adjust his traditional position as the interpreter of authoritarian ethics with the psychological principle of development in the emerging personality? How can he bring together, in a working relationship, a loyalty to deductive reasoning on the one hand, and a belief in revelation on the other? How is he to adjust the more directive mood of the pulpit with the more non-directive mood of the counseling room? Where does he as an individual find his true relationship to this dual function without destroying the integrity of his own growing personality?

These are the questions that are asked consciously or by indirection, whenever pastors come face to face with their tasks as counselors. Such questions reflect the nature of their mental training more than they indicate their own organization of life. For in a very real sense we cannot help living in two realms, and of responding to and being guided by forces that seem contradictory. As a ship at sea is subject to the material and non-material parts of its environment, so is the pastor in his work. The steel of the hull, the power of the screws and the surge of the waves seem the real ingredients of a sea voyage. But the captain on the bridge is also sensitive to another set of forces at work that are unseen and mysterious. The compass responds to unseen forces, the radio informs him through a controlled mystery, the stars in their courses supplement the compass, and the captain will not deny their reality, for he is dependent upon them. Adherence to these mysterious but reliable forces will determine his course and guarantee his safe arrival in harbor.

So the pastor is a captain in his own right, for he seeks to guide persons through the often uncharted waters of their own growth. He must be in control of the physical resources that are available, but he must also be responsive to those unseen and spiritual forces that play such an important part in the shaping of the human soul.

It is just at this dichotomy that Dr. Jung directs his criticism. "Among all my patients in the second half of life—that is to say, over thirty-five—there has not been one whose problem in the last resort was not that of finding a religious outlook on life. It is safe to say that everyone of them fell ill because he had lost that which the living religions of every age have given their followers, and none of them has been really healed who did not regain his religious outlook . . . Here, then, the clergyman stands before a vast horizon. But it would seem as if no one had noticed it. It also looks as though the Protestant clergyman of today is insufficiently equipped to cope with the urgent psychic needs of our age. It is indeed high time for the clergyman and the psychotherapist to join forces to meet this great spiritual task . . . It is from the clergyman, not the doctor that the sufferer should expect help."[1]

Here is the invitation for cooperative work in this field. But here is also a request to adopt a dual discipline that is not easy for the average clergyman. Dr. Jung made a study of why his patients did not go to a clergyman for help. He found that their answers fell into four groups, and indicated either an inability or unwillingness on the part of the clergy to try to adapt their approach to the discipline demanded by a scientific view of personality emergence. Let us look at the objections his patients raised, and try to evaluate them honestly.

In the first place, Jung said that his patients refused to seek help from their ministers because they considered them to be incompetent and inadequately trained in psychological matters. If this judgment of suffering souls is accepted at face value, what is to be said? Undoubtedly, there are at least three factors involved in this sort of judgment. There is the part of the truth which the patient exaggerates out of proportion. There is the inclination of the patient in our modern society to credit himself with a competence in such matters that he does not possess. And in the third place there is a difficulty on the part of the trained clergyman to make known his capabilities without involving himself in dubious professional practices.

The standards for training ministers in the arts of pastoral care are marked by a wide disparity. In schools with Bible-centered curricula, there is the probability that no attention will be given to psychology or pastoral counseling. Many schools for training ministers have nothing more than an introductory course on the techniques of counseling and pastoral care, with the assumption, valid or otherwise, that the student's college work should have given an adequate basis in psychology. But increasingly the major theological schools are placing more emphasis on this phase of the work, and are encouraging students to participate in the programs of clinical training that provide hospital experience. The military services have also made available in the Chaplain Corps helpful courses dealing with counseling and emotional problems.

The competence of pastors, by and large, when compared with other professional groups, should be judged favorably. Probably pastors read more books in this field than do doctors, lawyers, and other comparable professional groups. There are still evidences of disturbance within the medical profession between those who place a large emphasis on psychosomatic medicine and those who do not. The psychological knowledge of the lawyer is apt to be a pragmatism that he can apply directly to his work. The pastor, however, is involved in the sort of specific work with people that demands a wide interest in this field. He is concerned with the total person, and anything affecting the welfare of that total person in his business. The difficulty is apt to be that his reading is sporadic and not systematic. He is attracted by the latest book club selection in the field, and accepts its findings without an adequate background. This tends to give an unstable direction to his practice of pastoral care.

There is no doubt that it would be helpful for the average pastor to be able to have a training course each year that would help him to keep abreast of the developments in the field, and at the same time give him a background against which he could try to organize his independent study and experience. This sort of brief refresher course is made available through some of the more education-conscious denominations, but even these cannot take the place of an adequate and well-balanced seminary training in the field.

Then, too, one must consider the capacity of the individual pastor. Some men would be better counselors with no training than would others after a dozen courses, for some men have an innate concern for the common sense and healthy personalities of people, and other men do not. In working with pastors I find that there are some who say, "I don't know why it is but no one ever comes to me with his problems."

No simple course is apt to overcome the personality factors that put a distance between individuals. Some men express such immaturity, flippancy or coldness that a person hesitates to lay before such a one any deep problem. On the other hand, some men are so wholesome and genuine in their attitude toward others that they invite confidence and trust almost immediately.

The capacity of the individual pastor is probably determined largely by the quality of his own personality. It is difficult to cover up inadequacies in one's own personality, especially if one is not aware of them. I have been disturbed again and again at finding pastors whose approach to most human relations was a projection of some deep inner disturbance of their own. This almost automatically disqualified them for effective counseling relations with other persons. They merely spread the disturbance that was already within themselves.

For instance, the miracle worker who feels that he must solve everyone elses' problems for them is apt to project his own feeling of inadequacy, and the inevitable result is further frustration and failure. Similarly, the emotionally disturbed pastor who cannot keep himself from entering into the emotional experience of his counselee only adds to the problem that already exists. The same is true of the intellectually self-conscious individual who is afraid he may not know the answer, and so makes haste to bring to bear on the problem interpretations that are irrelevant, unnecessary, and usually dangerous for the welfare of the counselee.

Here as elsewhere, a little knowledge may be dangerous. I had a pastor come to me once, after a lecture, and indicate the success he had had with therapeutic hypnosis. I learned from him that he had seen a demonstration of hypnosis in a college classroom in psychology, and so felt capable of using it upon his parishioners. He had had no work in diagnosis, nor in counseling techniques. He did not seem to sense that hypnosis can be dangerous for the health of the personality in certain types of emotional disturbance. Nor did he seem to feel there was risk of certain reactions while the hypnotic trance was being induced, or during the trance, or during the post-hypnotic reaction. Certain reactions call for the most skilled handling. Such misuse of limited psychological information is dangerous and unwarranted. Even such well trained and qualified experts in the field as Leslie Weatherhead now feel that hypnosis is to be avoided as a technique in the pastoral counseling relationship.

Where the pastor is judged incompetent by his potential counselee, we may feel that this is a judgment predicated on his performance in the pulpit, or that it is the evidence drawn from his own personality, which has shown more signs of needing help than of giving it. This latter judgment may be emphasized by the fact that every move and attitude of the parish minister is a matter of public interest, whereas a psychiatrist or psychologist is able to protect the privacy of his personal life. When a pastor is judged competent, it is usually because he gives proof of health and maturity in his own personal and human relations, and because (and this can not be overemphasized) he breathes from his pulpit a sense of deep compassion and understanding.

Any person involved in the process of counseling has to contend with a mass of general misinformation and partial knowledge which leads the counselee to form judgments about himself and others that are unwarranted. The mass of superficial writing that is done in the area of so-called psychological information floods the popular press and leads the untrained to assume more understanding than is possible through such sources. Not only do they try to practice a weak form of self-analysis which is never satisfactory, but they proceed to give their interpretations of the behavior of others. Often this limited insight makes it more difficult to gain the type of insight that can change behavior and personality, because it leads to cynicism, arrogance, and an unfounded self-assurance.

To transfer this problem to the field of pure medicine,

147

we can see the dangers of self-diagnosis. A physician of my acquaintance recounted the following experience in his practice. A young woman, married five years and of unusual good health, became disturbed by recurring dizziness. She had been so well that she had not lost a day in the office in years, and could not see why she should now have such an indisposition. She had read enough to know that dizziness may be caused by eye disturbance, so she made an appointment with an eye specialist.

He charged her ten dollars for a careful examination of her eyes, but assured her she had no cause for disturbance as far as her eyes were concerned. She then reasoned that it might be her heart, and sought out a heart specialist who examined her heart thoroughly, charged her fifteen dollars and assured her that her heart was in perfect condition. Then in a mood of frank self-examination, she said to herself, "I am not one to fool myself. When my nerves get me down, I will not beat about the bush. I will go to a psychiatrist at once." And she did.

The psychiatrist examined her mental attitudes and emotional condition, charged her twenty-five dollars, and assured her that there was nothing about her condition that indicated further treatment by him. Having worked out her own chain of self-diagnosis, she found herself more distraught than ever.

At last she confided in her husband, whom she had been trying to protect from anxiety, and being an unimaginative sort of fellow, he suggested that she see their own family doctor. That night she went to the office of the general practitioner who knew her as a total person, and was aware that he appeared unglamorous to her because he specialized in nothing. After a brief examination he said, "You have nothing to worry about. Eat good wholesome food, get plenty of rest, and come see me in a month. You are pregnant, and your dizziness may be a factor in early pregnancy."

Our age of specialization has led to compartmentalized thinking. Persons who know little about medicine set themselves up as their own diagnosticians. Persons who know equally little about the state of their own souls take upon themselves the privilege of criticism of their pastor because of his dedication to two disciplines. Not only is he responsible to the scientific judgments concerning personality, but he is also responsible to the discipline that sees men and women as more than nerves, frustrations, and guilt complexes. It is his duty to see in them the eternal qualities of a human soul. With that approach he is inclined to see things that a psychologist would not see. He is not apt to be so directive in his approach, nor so dependent upon tests and projective methods in seeking an understanding. If a counselee does not understand the importance of the approach of this dual discipline, he is apt to be unreasonable in his criticism.

Here again, it may be the pulpit approach that helps to condition the thinking of the prospective counselee, but certainly the pastor cannot be obliged to accept responsibility for a trend that is prevalent in our day. The mood of specialization, the glamour of knowing more and more about less and less, is most evident in its weakness at the point where a person is unable to see himself wholly because he is so absorbed in meditating on his constituent parts.

Nor can we overlook the problems that are involved for the pastor who should make known any special professional ability or training that he may feel he has. When the new physician comes to town he can announce through normal channels that he is licensed to practice psychiatry. He can establish his relationship with various professional agencies within the community and thus guarantee his practice. He is recognized by others of the medical profession as a specialist in the field of mental illness, and through consultation and referral his professional status is established and maintained.

The pastor, however, is in quite a different position. He is not able to set up counseling relationships on a community or city-wide basis for he has a primary responsibility to his parish. It would be considered indiscreet of him to announce from the pulpit or through the church bulletin that he will be waiting for people to bring their problems to him at certain hours during the week. Good taste prevents the pastor from forcing himself into the personal affairs of his people. Too vigorous an effort to compel counseling situations can destroy the possibility of establishing a fruitful relation.

A pastor who had read enough of Freud to get the idea that most emotional problems are sex-centered, made it his practice to be alone with his charges as often as possible, so that he might inquire into the status of their sex life. His desire to be helpful (or was it a projection of his own problem?) made people afraid to be alone with him, and his chance to do effective work with people was severely limited. In the matter of establishing effective pastoral relations there are many things that a pastor cannot and should not do.

Yet there are important things he can do, and might well do as soon as possible after entering a parish. By his attitude and the investment of his time he may indicate the measure of significance he credits to pastoral care. Without fanfare he is able to indicate that he wants his people to feel that he is accessible at all times, and that as their pastor he does not want them to hesitate to call upon him when they feel he may be of service.

Through his program of pastoral calling, hospital visitation, and person-centered activities, he indicates his interest in the people of his parish. He may establish certain periods when people know he is in his office, and accessible to them. While he should guard against making his people feel that the only time they dare enter his office is when they enter with a problem, he should make any and all persons welcome when they do come for help. By his attitude toward his people he establishes his ability to act with dignity, to be worthy of confidence, and to be a wise listener.

Add to this a confident and kindly approach from the pulpit, with a sincere and sustained interest in seeing and meeting the spiritual needs of people, and the pastor will have gone a long way toward building a solid basis of pastoral counseling. Potential counselees will be less apt to decry his incompetence, and will increasingly look to him for help in time of need.

Another reason why patients were hesitant to approach a

Christian minister with their problems was—Dr. Jung found—their feeling that pastors would be condemnatory. In the patient's mind, at least, there is a confusion of the functions of prophet and pastor. The prophet condemns in order to prevent the consequences of sin. The pastor does not condemn in order to heal the consequences of conflict. And one would not be realistic if he believed that the conflict existed only in the mind of the potential counselee. The pastor himself often has difficulty in moving from the pulpit to the counseling room, just because he wants to carry with him the practice of preaching and condemning. A pastor cannot begin to function effectively in the counseling room until he is able to acknowledge his responsibility to two disciplines, and be able to shift gears, as it were, according to the needs of the situation.

The pastor's attitude towards sin will have much to do with his capacity to adjust to the two disciplines. If morality is for him a rigid adherence to a superimposed moral code, he will feel insecure when not operating in conformity with that code. He will feel that it is his mission to fix that code upon others, and will be unable to see the needs and rights of the counselee in any other terms. This sort of approach to morality is happily on the decline. For that is the morality of the scribes and pharisees, and not of the Master. Jesus saw sin as that which limited the chances for a more abundant life, and his function was to free life from those restraints. These restraints usually were not involved in the minutiae of the law but rather had to do with immaturity, restraints of love and spiritual power.

It would naturally be our desire to find guidance from

the teaching and practice of Jesus at this point. Here it seems his position is well defined. It was his practice never to condemn the sufferer who was in any way amenable to healing suggestion. When words of condemnation came from his lips they were directed toward those who by their action or possibly inaction were threatening the right to a more abundant life for others. Perhaps that is all the rule we need to escape the dangers of too rigorous an interpretation of moral codes. We can minister with patience and understanding and without condemnation as long as there is any possibility of effecting personality change through that approach. Because of our knowledge of the infinite possibilities within the human soul, we may largely discount the situations that might be exceptions to this rule.

As a matter of general practice I have tried to work out a simple basis that would prove effective in pastoral relations. Any set of rules immediately invites exception, but I have found these three simple ideas helpful in governing my relations with all persons.

First, to try never to say or do that which would limit my personal ministry. Even though situations might arise where persons would take offense at me, I should try to keep my attitude toward them free from resentment. This would keep a bridge across those inevitable human situations that develop where sharp differences of opinion must be expressed. Second, I try always to impute the highest possible motives to the actions of others. This keeps the "why" at the front of the mind, and seeks the most reasonable explanation for those things that seem unreasonable. It makes it possible to keep resentment at a minimum and understanding at its maximum. Third, I try to see the value of the person as a person, in whatever state he may be at the given moment. I have seen such remarkable transformation in persons that I no longer feel competent to pass a judgment where God has not.

Each pastor would want to work out his own personal basis for conduct, but he could establish for himself in the practice of counseling a far better approach if he kept close to the program of the Master, rather than to the restraints of a rigid moral code that tends to violate the very spirit of the Christ.

It is certainly well within the realm of effective practice to have and teach high moral standards, and at the same time work patiently and with understanding among those who have violated such a standard. It is those who are fearful of their own lack of inner resources who fear to associate with the needy in the healing process. Those with rich confidence and deep compassion can walk with publicans and sinners, gluttons and winebibbers, thieves and harlots, and remain pure and undefiled. For their first loyalty is to save the God-made souls of men rather than the man-made codes of behavior. Then pastors will be saved from an inclination to be condemnatory, and parishioners will feel free to approach them with troubles, without fear of having their already injured soul bruised even more by misunderstanding and condemnation. No one is healed by hatred and condemnation, and it was Jesus who said, "Judge not that ye be not judged."

The third reason Dr. Jung's patients gave for not wanting to go to a clergyman for help was that they expected the pastor to be shocked by their story. Little do some people realize the wide range of human experience a practicing pastor is obliged to share in the course of a year. If there is anything in human behavior, experience or trouble that he does not know, it is the exception. He has gone through the valley and the shadow of sin and suffering with many, and the more bizarre the human experience, the more apt he is to be involved in it eventually.

However, there is enough evidence of a shocked attitude in the reaction of some pastors to invite further exploration of the matter. Some pastors may feel obliged to act shocked to guarantee the purity of their own moral standards. They little sense what the raised eyebrow, the shocked attitude, and the clucking tongue may imply to the counselee.

In the first place an attitude of shock on the part of the counselor is an admission of rejection. In effect it says, "You offend me by what you say." The counselee may well be in trouble because he has been rejected so much, and has been made to feel a source of offense to so many. The moment he feels further rejected by the counselor, all effort to seek healing for his soul, to find light for his inner darkness, and to find a sense of self-revelation for his unsolved mysteries of behavior, are nipped in the bud, and he goes away defeated.

Expression of shock is an expression of unconscious antipathy. Self revelation in the atmosphere of friendly understanding may be a spiritual cleansing. Shock says, "I want no part in helping to clean up the rottenness of your soul." If the shocked attitude leads to a sermon, the effect is to further "brush off" the individual. It effectively adds insult to injury. It is a refusal to grant the love and compassion that are needed to let the festering soul bring to a head its infection. It expresses a fear of contamination that not only reveals low resistance, but also indicates a small capacity for empathy and reassurance. This in effect tells the counselee that the counselor is incapable and inadequate for the task before him.

The pastor's task often is to do very little but listen. If there is any inclination to be shocked, blot it out. Then the troubled soul will be able to open up and respond. The sufferer will feel loved and helped and healed.

The pastor who feels shocked is not actually passing a moral judgment, he is revealing an area of his own ungoverned emotions. The pastor whose concern for people is genuine and deep is shockproof as far as the words and acts of the counselee are concerned, and he is thus able to be effective as an instrument in God's hands in the healing process. For the shockproof attitude helps to ventilate and cleanse, as it brings about self revelation and exteriorizes that which had proved to be a source of spiritual infection. The shocked attitude is one of rejection, antipathy, and incompetence. The ability to see the person beyond the disturbing experiences of life is evidence of compassion, forebearance and love.

The final complaint of Dr. Jung's patients about the pastors they knew, or thought they knew, was that they already knew what would be said. Here of course, they immediately associate the pastor with his public speaking, the one who traditionally is a "sayer" if not a "soothsayer." They expect from him only the traditional theology and the authoritarian ethics. These they think they know and so judge them inadequate for their needs, and they are probably right.

One of the barriers they indicate is language. Many of the things the preacher talks about are in effect a foreign language to the listener. He knows the words have something to do with religion, but it is a jargon so far removed from his daily experience that it is almost the same as "talking in tongues."

The pastor who would overcome such objections should be careful about the use of words in the pulpit. He would try to reveal rather than obscure. He would clarify rather than befog. I have noticed that those who do considerable counseling are inclined to use rather simple direct speech in their pulpits. The effect is casual, and the listeners feel drawn by the words of one who speaks with simplicity and understanding. He is understood and so is considered to be understanding. In like manner, the Ivory Tower approach, with words of erudition far above the heads of the listeners, creates an effect of separation. "He may be a wonderful preacher, but he is not talking to me," the listener says, and goes elsewhere for help with his soul needs.

A frank facing of the judgments of those who refuse to seek aid for their souls from the traditional soul-healers, the clergy, can give us pause. There is enough truth about the statements to keep us on guard against the practices that interfere with a most effective pastoral relationship. Yet there is much the people have to learn about the adequacy of their clergy before they pass a judgment upon themselves in the process. The clergyman is still the one soul healer who seeks the total person—mind, body, and spirit, instincts, emotions, and reason. He it is who is obliged to be responsive to the scientific judgments of personality without being limited by the scientific view of spiritual values.

The pastor's honest effort to see people with scientific interest as well as spiritual understanding may make him best fitted not only to work with people, but also ready for the further scientific understanding that will illuminate the power of the human spirit to achieve greater heights than now attained. The researches of the para-psychologists, the psychic researchers and even the biochemists and astrophysicists are developing new concepts of matter and spirit, that may well transform the view of man and the universe. The pastor still sees people as the children of the living God, and heirs of life eternal. His work with them must always be conditioned by this larger view of the life that can be ever more and more abundant.

Two disciplines that at first seem to be contradictory become one through a cultivated awareness and an all pervading concern for what happens to persons in the totality of their living. Person-centered preaching creates the atmosphere that leads to effective pastoral care at all levels of the parish ministry.

8

HOW JESUS PREACHED

*I*T WOULD SEEM that the circumstances surrounding the preaching of Jesus were so different from those
that engage us now that there could be only contrast. However there are important points in content and method
which show a close relationship. The message of Jesus

is still our message. The concern for persons is still our concern. So let us take a closer look at the content and method of preaching employed by Jesus as a source of guidance for our main message and major concern.

The materialistic view of life measures life by death. The spiritual view evaluates death by life. And there lies the core and purpose of Christian preaching, for it is our goal to build life by revealing one who is both the resurrection and the life.

The abundant life we would set as the goal of Christian living is not a denial but a fulfillment. It is a maturity and a power and a love that are inseparably bound together. When one finds life, he finds all three. Yet often the church has made itself the guardian of limitations upon life, so that it stands for denial, useless sacrifice, and a rejection of the very attitudes that could make life most real. Just as it is always easier to be immature than mature, so is it also easier to negate than to affirm, to deny rather than to fulfill.

But ours is a positive message, a declaration of life that is abundant. In our day, with its denials and its repudiation of life through a persistent dedication to war methods, this message of life can be especially inviting. Youth faced by the demands of their society for military service and early death find a challenge in this message of life. Parents faced with the loss of all they had worked to build find hope in the message that is both life and peace. It is time for the church, which is the custodian of this way of life, to be done with denials, with efforts to rationalize, or with easy compromise. Why should we seek reasons for a just war when we have reasons for a just life? Why should we seek justification for a society that makes selfishness a goal and concern a by-product, when we can declare a way of life that makes concern a goal and selfishness a contradiction?

"Before a quiet church that smells of death." This is the phrase Don Marquis used in one of his poems to describe the church as too many people see it. Because it has feared to speak a virile message of life, it has come to be the place for funerals and the center of a burial ground. But in recent years the commercial interest of the funeral home has superseded the church. Perhaps the Master's invitation to "let the dead bury the dead" has found an acceptance that could jar our consciousness. One does not usually look to Swinburne for an accurate portrait of a preacher, but perhaps he has come closer than we would want to admit in this line from an unpublished manuscript, "For tender minds, he served up half a Christ."

We probably do an injustice to the minds of our hearers if we think they cannot stand the truth. We usually think of men of money as wanting "to pay the preacher and call the tunes," but I heard a few weeks ago of a millionaire who was seeking a minister for his church who would not "just tell us what we want to hear, but would tell us what we ought to know." Many of the more honest and intelligent among our businessmen are aware of the limitations on their understanding of human and social dynamics. They can see the direction in which human and social and national affairs are moving. They are as zealous as anyone for a way of life to lead them beyond what seems to be an inevitable doom.

161

Our task then is not to try to be an interpreter of the details of business or social forces, though we should know all we can about them. Ours is the task of making Jesus live again in sharp relief before our people, so that they can see the most mature, the most powerful, and the most love-dominated personality of history. How may our task be achieved? How can we use the possibility for group therapy that a sermon affords to speak the healing words of Life? How can we overcome the limitation that speaking to a variety of persons, of a variety of ages and interests, places upon us? How can we help each of our people in the process of growth toward a more abundant life and a more abounding personality?

One might study the words and method of Jesus for the answers to these questions. For Jesus was a master at the devices of direct appeal to the attention and response of his hearers. He was simple in his presentation. No one from the child to the scholar could be confused by what he said. He used stories that were related to the experience of his hearers, and each story had one main point that stood out too clearly to be mistaken.

The listener's interest is guaranteed by a plentiful use of narrative material. Not only does this serve the purpose of keeping the interest, but it also serves a more important psychological purpose of making it possible for the hearer to identify himself with the characters of the story and live himself through the incidents. Then he is conditioned emotionally as well as intellectually for similar situations when they arise in his own experience.

Jesus was not afraid to be personal and declarative. He

knew that it was important for hearers to know whether or not the speaker believed what he said, or whether he was just talking. The ability to make his person a part of his message made the message live. For Christianity cannot be separated from the person of Jesus, and effective preaching cannot be divorced from the person of the preacher. Jesus could make theology simple: "I and the Father am one." He could make ethics simple: "Which of these three was a neighbor?"

Never was the message left dangling, unrelated to life. If it were a life situation, there was a need for response. "Let him who is without sin cast the first stone." If it were a parable, it implied or directed action. "Go and do thou likewise." If it were a pastoral call, it involved something more than a pleasantry. "Come, follow me." If it were an illustration, it carried its alternatives that demanded a mental participation. "Which of these two went down to his house justified?" "He who heareth my word and doeth it is like the man who built upon the rock."

Jesus felt that the object of talking with people was to communicate something of himself and of his heavenly Father. That method was best which served best. So he achieved a mastery of the speech of the people. So he communicated himself. So he still serves as an example to his followers of pulpit speech and method that can open doors to the more abundant life.

How better could one portray the need for maturity of spirit than to make the differing types of maturity and immaturity stand up and be seen. This Jesus did with his parable of the Mature and Immature men, commonly

163

known as the Good Samaritan. With what sharp lines he portrays the immaturity of the lawyer who retreats into intellectuality as a defense against responsible action. How clearly we can see that lawyer and his type as they hedge and ask questions and look for some loop-hole in the divine logic of life. For them the mind is an instrument to confuse rather than to reveal the truth. For them the mental legerdemain of the sophist takes the place of a sincere desire to know life. Such is the immature mind that would limit its power to act and its capacity to love.

Where has the immaturity of piety been shown better than by the clearly etched figure of the priest? "When he saw he passed by." He had the capacity to see but it meant nothing. He had built a cocoon of piosity about himself so tightly that there was no longer room for a healthy emotion. He probably practiced celibacy and tithed his salt and pepper and thought that made him good. He had damned up the wells of human feeling until they no longer existed and he could walk by human suffering as blithely as if it did not exist. Such religion is an evidence of the ends to which life may go to protect its immaturity and avoid those responsibilities that go with maturity. What blasphemy can be done in the name of God, and what courage it took for a story-teller to draw such bold characterizations.

Who does not feel the life-stifling influence of petty occupation as the Levite is torn between his better impulses and his slavery to a belittling routine? A custodian of the Temple, how important he felt his task to be. His involvement with the symbols of religion kept him from practicing the nature of religion. He was moved to come closer and

164

look, but his life was bound by devotion to lesser things. His was the immaturity that loses the big things in a maze of little things. His was the impotence of feeling that possesses the persons who escape into a job to be free of the responsibility of living. Can you not see yourself as you take refuge in some trivial appointed task rather than declare your freedom for the larger act of living. Yes, little responsibility can take the place of big responsibility. Trivial living can be the escape from the more abundant life.

How mature a picture of life Jesus builds through his portrayal of the neutral figure of the unidentified man who fell among thieves. Not a word is mentioned concerning his race, or his nationality, or his station in life. No indication is given as to his religion or his habits or practices. He merely lies there by the road, the symbol of the innate value of a man, whose only merit was his membership in the family of God, the human race. What insight of the Master left this man so unidentified, for even the word "certain" in this sense means uncertain. Yet this claim of a man in need could not be escaped. It was the testing point of everyone else in this story. He became the boundary marking the line between the mature and the immature by the very nature of their response to his inert form.

It is difficult to appreciate the boldness of the Master's choice of a Samaritan for the hero's spot in this story. The Samaritan was of all persons the least regarded. He was a social, political and racial outcast. In our society it is not easy to think of an equivalent. Yet when he came to the fallen man he acted with a sense of maturity. He gave the first aid to the bruised body. Then he accepted responsibility for the man's welfare during an interim period that would be involved prior to the return of strength and independence. Not only did he take him to an inn, but he gave a guarantee for whatever else might be needed to restore the man to normal life again. He met the test of the highest type of maturity, that of unlimited and unrestrained compassion. Perhaps our Master was here indicating his own relationship to the intellectual and religious and social groups of his day. By the final testing, they were tried in the balance and found wanting. But the lowly Samaritan met the Master's dimensions for a man.

Nor can we overlook the maturity of the "forgotten man" of the story, the innkeeper. His was a life of service, and he was set to take the good and the ill who came along this road. His was a haven of warmth and nourishment and even nursing care for those who were in need. There is no evidence that he carried on a "restricted" business. He was there to serve, and when the time came he did not make excuses. How easily he could have begged off by saying he was not set up to run a hospital, asking how was he sure that he would get his board and room. He took the injured man on faith and ministered to his needs. In so doing he ranks as a hero in the story, of perhaps a lower rank, but hero indeed. He met a life situation without effort to escape. He accepted his responsibility with maturity.

The maturity of the narrator is revealed by the courage and clarity of his characterizations, for the story is undoubtedly a matter of self-revelation. He did not need to tell the story, nor did he need to tell it as he did. But he presented it in this direct and simple fashion so that no one could miss the movement and direction of the story. When all had had a chance to see its meaning, he turned it back upon them with a question that they could not avoid answering, and in so doing commit themselves. But he did not leave it with the question alone. With two of the simplest but most demanding words of any language, he put the whole burden of the story upon those who would practice the escapes of immaturity. "Go and do."

Thus our Master uses the simple, direct, and declarative narrative to draw a picture of the mature approach to life. It is the approach of power equal to the emergencies of life. It is the approach of love that is not deflected by clever devices of mind or emotion, but is true to its larger nature. So our Master revealed himself and his God who was Love in unmistakable terms. After hearing Jesus speak, men might still be free to say "Yes" or "No," but they were certainly not free from themselves, for they could not help seeing the problem of life and their own relation to it.

St. Paul realized that the struggle for maturity was no easy thing. He said that "when he became a man he put away childish things," but he also admitted that even now "we see through a glass darkly," and "what I would do I do not, and what I would not do that I do." He was well aware of the fact that maturity is more than an ideal, for it is a discipline of living that demands concentration and dedication. Much of the trouble people get into is a result of immature thought and behavior on the adult level. Surely our bodies cease growing and our minds acquire a measure of maturity, but it is the emotional growth that is so apt to have strange ties to the childhood past. The problems of emotional immaturity are not to be solved until the personality recognizes them for what they are. Then they must be led on to a new level of behavior, built upon a new consciousness of responsibility.

Jesus knew well that emotions do not grow by advice, or by an appeal to the very weaknesses that already exist. He would have had little sanction for the preacher who made his main appeal to the obsessive-compulsive personality by giving petty formulas of superficial behavior as a door to new life. He would have resented the preacher who used an authoritarian approach to fasten to him those maiden ladies, married and unmarried, who wanted a father to tell them what to do, rather than accept their obligation to grow to the place where they could stand on their own two feet. The same would apply to those guilty sons whose unresolved childhood emotions made them crave a father's chastisement. Nor would Jesus have looked with favor on the pulpit Pied Pipers who lead their followers into blind alleys of emotionalism or vapid sentimentalism when they are in need of a maturity that can lead them to adult behavior and a demanding sentiment. The pulpit practice of appealing to already warped personalities by taking advantage of the very weaknesses that warped them is not only unexcusable ignorance but a cruel perversion of the sadist's mind.

Jesus knew that personalities could be led to grow by the leaven of suggestion. The timid trout is not pulled from the stream by loud noise and by flailing the water. Rather, it responds to the quiet descending of the unsuspected fly. The fisher of men cannot forget that souls are timorous and must be approached without bold assault upon their innermost sanctuaries. He it was who acted the perfect gentleman with every soul, never prying but always supporting each human effort to grow. When he was ruthless it was with the growth preventing force. His tenderness with that which grew from within was a lesson in love and patience.

A sermon may be rich in suggestion without creating an offense to the growing spirit by too authoritarian demands. A sermon may present alternatives so graphically that the hearer cannot but see himself in relation to inevitable choices. When choices are made in advance in theoretical situations, they are made more easily in actuality when life situations develop. But there is a marked difference between the alternative presented with condemnation and the alternative presented with a sense of empathy that makes the hearer feel the right choice is made winsome through a genuine concern and friendship.

The Master's approach never violated a sense of reality. He did not demand the impossible or create unreal situations. He did not minimize suffering or ignore sin. Rather would he use suffering for creative purposes, for he knew that suffering has power. He tried to teach his hearers to use suffering creatively. When, on the way to the cross he heard the weeping of those who lined the Via Dolorosa, he said "Weep not for me but for yourselves." He knew how to suffer creatively, but he realized that their suffering was impotent and destructive.

It is no mystery to us that suffering is power. We see those who suffer and are unbroken grow in spiritual stature, for they have increased their compassion, understanding and love. We can build life by an honest facing of its realities. We can invite those who suffer to find its meaning in a larger context, so that their suffering becomes not an end but a means toward an end. It is not whether or not life has Gethsemanes, but what is done with them that counts. It is not that life should escape the crosses, but rather that it should use the crosses creatively. Power is generated within the soul not by withdrawal from life, or removal of its inevitable burdens, but by redirecting the emotional energy of suffering so that it becomes creative power instead of power to destroy.

There is a cheapness to easy reassurance that is obvious to all concerned. There is a power of the mind that opens doors to larger meaning. "Come unto me all ye that labor and are heavy laden and I will give you rest. Take my yoke upon you and learn of me, for my yoke is easy and my burden is light." Rest is a break in labor, not a cessation of it. A yoke is not a denial of work but an instrument for making work more effective. Jesus does not deny the burden, but he indicates how it may be readjusted and lightened. The sermon that seeks a popular appeal through an escape from the realities of life is a step on the road to disillusionment. The sermon that faces the reality of life and presents the alternatives for its creative usefulness helps the personality to grow in stature as it grows in grace.

There is a mysterious creativeness about life itself. There is a reserve of power that we can easily overlook. The message of AA is one concerning the reservoirs of untapped power within the soul of the alcoholic. I have seen those who followed the road of destructive power to its end and found nothing. I have seen them after they have trod the road back standing with power and conviction making their witness for a new way of life. Yes, committed to the alcoholic ward in Bellevue Hospital forty-two times, and now, thanks to a constructive use of new found power, living a sober and useful life. I have seen criminals, in and out of jail for years, standing before the community with dignity and self-respect because they have found a saving power within themselves that responded to the saving power of God's love for them. Jesus sought to release the power of God's kingdom within his hearers. It was life, and it was power and it was maturity.

There is power in failure when it is accepted with maturity. The compulsive neurotic needs to learn to fail. The quest for a meaningless perfection in inconsequentials destroys the life of such a person. He needs to learn the true meaning of a Gethsemane and a Cross. He needs to understand that the best laid plans can abort without destroying life. It may take a Patmos experience to create the vision of an Apocalypse. It may take the disappointment of a Troas to open the doors to a Macedonia. One of the measurements of growth is the ability to accept deprivation creatively. The master of bereavement is not the one who feels no sense of loss. Rather it is the person who has placed limits on his own selfish interests so that he is not shattered by the realities that cannot be avoided. Ultimately, each failure presents new alternatives. It can be a door to growth in personality, or it can be a signal for a retreat into a haven of immaturity. A sermon that grows out of understanding of people, and a firm sense of reality, can help men to grow from experience to experience with an increase of maturity and emotional health. It is a weekly challenge to growth, and a persistent stimulus to creative choice.

There is real power in the ability to value other people for their own sakes. Much immaturity that causes conflict in personal affairs grows out of the inability to value others except as they can be used for selfish purposes. Such is the persistent problem of the neurotic individual. He sees others as reflections of himself rather than as distinct other personalities. Such being the case he projects his inner conflicts upon others. If he doubts himself, he is suspicious of others. If he has fear within, he adds to it the fear of others. If he has a sense of guilt, he is quick to condemn others. His sense of reality breaks down because he can see nothing but himself. That is the state of immaturity you expect in a baby but not in an adult. When such immaturity is a part of life it sets impossible demands on life and makes neurotic failures inevitable. The healthy soul, however, values life in its goals and in the process of achieving them. He enjoys life and the living of it. He enjoys the home he builds and he enjoys the task of building it. He enjoys his family and friends, and does not expect perfection, for he senses that they are growing persons as he is. He knows their problems and their interests, and is able to enter into their joys and sorrows because he values them for what they are, other souls. A sermon can be the instrument to awaken an understanding and appreciation of others that will help to dissolve and adjust the problems of interpersonal relations that immaturity builds.

Faith has power to dispel fear. A characteristic of our age is a spiraling fear that increasingly involves our total way of life. We are told that unless we respond in kind to the actions of our alleged enemies we will be destroyed. Yet no one tells us that our own fear is destroying us more rapidly than any forces from without. We are custodians of a way of life that believes in God. It is the communists who should stand in fear, for they have bowed God out of their world. They cannot be on the winning side ultimately, for they have denied the spiritual nature of life. Even the atom bomb has declared against their interpretation of materialism. We are on the winning side if we are on God's side. If we would give more time and energy to seeking God's will we would find a reserve of spiritual power to sustain us in the process. If we deny our faith, and adopt the methods and attitudes of those who abhor the faith we espouse, we cannot expect to achieve any real victory. If our preaching is so filled with denunciations of athiests that we find no place for a positive development of our spiritual life, we have done our people and our message an injustice. Probably the pulpit is the one place in our world today where men can be called to a vision beyond that inspired by fear and falsehood. Let us not fail to use the privileges this historic moment gives us to declare a faith large enough for men to build a better world upon.

So often we fail to sense that the devices in general practice to promote nationalism and acceptance of a war psychology are the very attitudes that prevent objective judgment and a rational understanding of the dynamics of peoples and nations. The more we practice those attitudes that limit love, the more difficult is it for us to release the healing power of love in life. Love is like a window while falsehood and hate are like mirrors. I stopped into the Chamber of Mirrors in Versailles Palace where the Treaty of Versailles had been signed. All that I could see on every side was myself. I became a multitude. When I became everything, all horizon was gone and so was all perspective. What a deadly monotony when self is everywhere. How different it was a few days later when I climbed a tower in the mountains with unobscured windows on every side. There were far vistas on every side with mountains and plains, cities and villages filled with people and life. How refreshing to see so much. How insignificant I felt, and how proper my relationship became to all else.

Sermons can help persons preoccupied with self to see beyond to those relationships than can nourish and strengthen self. The self becomes a menace when it lives unto itself. The mentally ill are often those who are obsessed with self. But outreach gives health of mind and emotion. It opens new depths within the soul of the one who learns the mature responsibility that goes with right relations with others. And in turn there is that greater reward of fellowship that sustains the life of the mature individual in home and church and community. The lonely soul is the self-centered soul. The mature soul is the one that is not separated from his fellows, but rather responds to them with a full measure of appreciation and understanding. He is civilized, as only the demands of Christianity, the most civilized state of being, can make him. New channels for spontaneity and enthusiasm grow within the man who grows rich in his associations with those who can inspire and enrich his living through a mature communion of mind and heart.

A sense of purpose brings power to life. The preacher's words can be potent in making clear life's meaning and purpose, and releasing the power that can be organized about a worthy goal. The story is told of a football game between the University of Southern California and Notre Dame in which it was quite obvious that the western college was outclassed. Early in the game the team from Notre Dame made two touchdowns, and then placed their second team in the game. Using all of their energy the Pacific Coast team was able to hold the second team without further score. During the half it seemed to the coach that there was nothing to be said to his team for they had done their best, but were just outplayed. But suddenly there was a commotion in the locker room, and a strikingly beautiful young woman burst into the room. With tears in her eyes and voice she said, "Men, you must win this game for my dying brother. He is an alumnus of this school, and is listening. He will be gone in a few days, but will die content if this game is won. You must win for him." When they went onto the field for the second half they were a different team. To be sure, they weighed the same, and a picture would have indicated that they were the same persons. But something had happened to them, and Notre Dame knew it, when these men who had been outclassed before now played as if they were inspired. The game was won, not because of their outstanding ability, but because they had an inspiring sense of purpose.

A sermon can take the struggling life that seems burdened beyond endurance, and give it a new direction, a new purpose so that it goes out to face the world with released power. There is no congregation but feels the life of a word of inspiration. There is no burdened life but can readjust its burden with a new sense of the reason why burdens are borne. Somber indeed is the service that has no place for that word of encouragement than can sharpen the purpose of living, and help each worshipper to place a higher value upon his own existence.

Jesus was able to meet the most severe situations and bring out unused resources. Skipping the problems of scholarship in the story of the Gaderene demoniac, we find the Master approaching a suffering outcast. His approach was normal and calm. He did the thing anyone would do by making inquiry as to his name. When the man explained the nature of his problem, he urged order upon his confused personality. Instead of the torment and fear that was a part of his life, he was met with kindness and calmness, and he became a new man, clothed and in his right mind.

While our congregations will not usually have marked personality disturbances in their midst, they will always have those who are confused and fearful, who feel the civil war of contending purposes within themselves. The word of insight that can help them to bring a truce to their strife because they have accepted a common loyalty to a higher purpose, gives a chance for a life of greater usefulness and happiness. They can be whole again, and words from the pulpit can be the instruments in creating that wholeness.

Since the advent of the psychiatrist, the significance of words has gained scientific acceptance. Words are now generally accepted as tools to operate on souls that are afflicted. Words are the medicine that can start at work the spiritual chemistry that can bring about a new balance within the personality. Words are the catalytic agent that can precipitate a new reaction to life in the individual. Words have gained new stature as means of saving life. That which the pulpit has always felt to be true has been sustained by the judgment and practice of those who are dedicated to a scientific view of personality. And strangely enough, they bend their words to the task of bringing to the sick soul a sense of maturity, a release of power, and a capacity to fulfill the needs for love in their own living.

So after struggling in the throes of controversy and experimentation for fifty years, the champions of a scientific view of personality arrive at the same conclusions as those who enunciated a new way of life two thousand years ago. They are seeking to do what the pulpit at its best has tried to do through the centuries. Ours, however, is the great debt, for we can now add understanding to the intuition that has blessed the few great pulpit masters—the understanding that can enrich the approach of all. For much that has been done in the pulpit has been little more than a projection of the disturbances and maladjustments of the preacher himself. We now know enough to make that sort of thing forever inexcusable. We are now obliged to develop that maturity within the pulpit that will cultivate a maturity within the pew, where in the past the opposite has been all too often true. The maturity of the pew has with patient tolerance endured the immaturity of the pulpit, and with a fine wisdom winnowed the wheat of the words from the chaff of the hate, fear, and impotence of the immature spokesman of the Lord.

When the words from the pulpit are obviously the effort of a person-conscious pastor to mediate the healing love of God, he will open the doors of people's hearts, as well as open the doors to his counseling room. For effective preaching will always be an invitation to go further in the exploring of personal needs. Here then, the problem is not one of pulpit polish or erudition of phase and literary allusion, but rather the capacity to feel the needs of others and meet those needs. The quatrain of Henry Van Dyke might well be framed on the study wall of most ministers:

> He who seeks for heaven alone to save his soul
> May keep the path but will not reach the goal,
> While he who walks in love may wander far,
> But God will bring him where the blessed are.

When God's redeeming love is made operative in life, the chains of fear and guilt and remorse that bind so many to the past will be broken, and a new flood of power will direct life toward a future of vital usefulness. Then the past can be made to work for the future, rather than against it. Then what can be done is evaluated against what cannot be undone. Before the Archives Building in Washington, Robert Aitken has sculptured a seated figure of a woman with a large book in her lap. It is opened to the

178

last pages. On the pedestal of the statue are chiseled these words, "All that is past is prelude. The Future begins now."

Something in the words of each sermon may well suggest that there is a release of power for those who sense the privilege of the future more than the burden of the past. The sin of the past loses much of its power for those who refuse to be governed by it. It remains a vicious slave master of those who remain chained to it.

The release of God's power in life is not a dialectic. It is an experience. The pulpit's task is never finished until it has given some kind of an invitation to "taste and see that the Lord is good." All of the knowledge of electricity possible does not bring the result of simply turning a switch. All the knowledge of God does not equal the effect of living one day in faith and love. For the pulpit not only tries to give the knowledge and make clear its meaning; it seeks to inspire a venture of life that will accept the discipline of released power and love. Knowledge must be fulfilled in action. Jesus came to fulfill and to help men to fulfill. This calls for living inside the faith, rather than merely pursuing it from the outside.

My first view of Notre Dame was disappointing, for from the outside it seemed somber and forbidding. But when I had entered the portals, and felt the surge of its uplifting lines, and saw the beauty of the color of the windows from within, it was a new experience. The calm, quiet dignity of every line led to worship. The experience from within was a new and different appreciation. Ours is the task of helping to create the experience that feels the power of religion from within.

Many souls are dead or dying. Ours is a message of life. Many men do not realize their own needs. Ours is to make them aware. Ours is to substitute real goals for the false gods. Ours is to take the church that "smells of death" and make it breathe life.

A modern poet, Don Marquis, has in a few lines indicated the spiritual health of too many of our contemporaries.

> To and fro about the town
> The dead men hurry up and down,
> Whirling corpses, moving dust,
> Driven of gold and greed and lust,
> Filmy eyes and grey of cheek,
> How they babble, bite and squeak.
> But these dead men take no thought
> Of things that are not sold and bought,
> In their bodies there is breath,
> But their souls are steeped in death.

We preach Christ, and for such souls this is a source of "resurrection and life." The preacher is an instrument in God's hands, to see, to feed, to guide, and to love God's children into life.

9

IN CONCLUSION

*T*HESE PAGES have been primarily concerned with the techniques of preaching. We have tried to explore psychological insights as they apply to personal and group processes. But we have tried never to lose sight of the art through preoccupation with technique.

181

Before we conclude we would take a few moments to re-emphasize the importance of preaching as an art form which can be enriched by insights from many sources but always preserves for itself those qualities that owe more to the mysteries of inspiration than to the disciplines of technical mastery. The art is the creative mastery of the methods the medium affords. But the purpose of the art form directs its use.

The art of Christian preaching is rooted in absolutes and expressed in paradoxes. Strange it may seem to speak of absolutes in a day when relativity dominates popular thinking in so many diverse fields, yet the long view shows certain qualities of preaching which have stood out through hundreds of years, and stand now. Purpose, truth, sincerity, critical insight and human sympathy are ingredients that must be added to technical mastery in achieving what is an art.

We speak of the art of preaching. What meaning has the term for us? Do we think of a formal presentation in spoken words where special care is given to the turning of a phrase, strings of glittering adjectives are at a premium, and scintillating sentences sparkle sumptuously? Or do we mean that type of message which is burdened with truth and fitted for the human heart which will come under its influence? Or do we, perchance, think of the union of the two as that surpassing achievement of the mind of a sensitive man who knows God and man well enough to make art serve its rightful purpose?

Michelangelo stretched his medium until it writhed in overborne meaning. A hundred years later the French

IN CONCLUSION

Academy was eagerly seeking the secret of the great master's power. Poussin, the father of the Academy, copied the style and method of Michelangelo with unusual skill, but with him a carefully studied technique took the place of spontaneity. The technical perfection of the work could not replace the power and meaning of the master's emotional strength and vitality.

A mere mode of artistic execution always falls short of the meaning gained through an electrically charged emotion which finds expression through technical perfection. The emphasis of the processes of attaining perfection became so assertive that the communicative and meaningful element of the art was pushed almost entirely out of sight. The artists lost their appreciation of the natural basis for everything ideal, and the ideal fulfillment of everything natural. In doing so their art became stilted and petty. Art is a language, and dies when it carries no meaning. The consummatory expression and the communicative value are essential to each other. One is the result of the formation of the idea in the mind of the creator, the other is the presentation in a way that has significance to the appreciator. A picture with no meaning is similar to a language whose words are devoid of symbolism. Similarly a picture that has meaning, but presents it without significant form, is like a story told by a mute. What is an artful sermon in the light of contrast?

A few days after Emerson had sent a book of essays to press, he wrote in his Journal, "When I look at the sweeping sleet amid the pine trees, my sentences look very contemptible, and I think I will never write more: but the

183

words prompted by an irresistible charity, the words whose path from the heart to the lips I cannot follow,—are fairer than the snow. It is pitiful to be an artist." In a few words the Concord thinker and lover of men touched the heart of the art of preaching. Humility, a heart and a mouth—how they work together!

A man must stand before nature and God. As his knowledge of nature and man and God grows, so does his humility. As he sees and sympathetically appreciates man, his heart yearns, and his tongue burns. "It is pitiful to be an artist."

Who will deny that it is in the face of such trial and testing that preaching really becomes great? The heart of any art is the overcoming of difficulties in the medium for the sake of the meaning. In preaching as with all arts, the intelligent use of the medium is essential, the emotional dynamic of the burning heart gives purpose and direction to the intelligence, but the tongue must also burn with direction. A piece of marble or a strip of canvas may carry its message for centuries, but the spoken word dies the moment it is uttered unless it ignites the thinking of the congregation with sparks of meaning. In the L'Oiseau du Feu, Stravinsky illustrates the arrival of the fire bird. In a wild and barbaric orgy of musical sound the bird swoops down out of the clouds to dart flaming feathers over the landscape. As each feather ignites the spot upon which it lands, the music bursts out in many different flaming passages, but as the conflagration grows the consuming fire becomes one tremendous blaze of music. So in artful preaching the spoken words must drop from the mouth of the preacher as feathers of fire to kindle the hearts of the hearers and unite all in one flaming passion for the good, true, and beautiful.

The sermon must drive with all power toward one point. It must have a theme, a center of concentration and a point of focus. There are many ways of presenting a theme. One might do as Herman Melville did in *Moby Dick*—characterize one man, and through him express a whole philosophy. Ishmael draws into himself the world-view of Melville.

A sermon through its central theme can be the expression of the thinking of the preacher, and the use of one particular character may be the vehicle of so doing. Or, the fugal type of sermon may be used to arrive at the same end with a different approach. Built on the plan of a Bach perfect fugue, it may present first the exposition, the direction of thought, and then with skill and variation bring the same idea back in varying places and combinations, until at the end the masterly stretto gathers up all of the meaning and presents it in one passionate climax. This type demands the use of varying illustrations with taste and reserve. The former requires a strong central character to carry the burden of the idea within himself.

Almost as important as the theme is the thematic variation. No person can concentrate for thirty or forty minutes. His interest must be carefully shifted for him from one subject to another which is related to and supports the main theme. We see a very good example of this method in the variation form of music. A main theme is presented in numerous musical variations, sometimes embellished, sometimes practically indistinguishable, often by modulations into another key or through change of range. The melodic line remains the same, but the idea is varied to demand the most of it. In a sermon the text and central idea must remain, but the embellishments, the variations and degrees of intensity may cover a wide range. Instead of weakening the sermon, this tends to keep the mind of the listener more keenly aware of the idea. Also it makes accessible to more people an idea which they might not comprehend in a one-way presentation.

The balance of a sermon is the proper equalizing of the theme and thematic variation. Only sensitivity to aesthetic values and meanings can determine this.

One cannot pass lightly over the importance of the dramatic element in a sermon. By this I mean the unity of a process by which the earlier parts determine the later outcome. It is the evolution we see in a play, a novel or a Beethoven symphony. The development may take two directions—it may be unqualifiedly dramatic, or it may be a thorough, logical development that appeals so directly and forcefully to the mind that the unfolding of the thought creates its own intensity.

In a written form this latter type might be exemplified in *The Education of Henry Adams*. We can almost tell what is coming next, but the unraveling of his life as he steps along majestically, quietly and reverently is so intriguing that one follows with almost the keen delight a drama draws forth.

Surrounding and dominating all else must be the unity of the sermon. Every part must serve a purpose, nothing must be there which is not needed, and nothing should be omitted which is required. The central force in every work of art is unity of expression. Music, the dance, decorating, canvas and pigment, marble and the chisel, stress and balance, poetry, drama, prose and a sermon are kindred in their purpose as arts. But where is the sermon distinctive?

Each art is an attempt of man to give expression to the transcendent meaning of life as he sees it. Each sermon is, or should be, an attempt to interpret life in terms of the transcendent meaning one achieves through religion. As any age without art is poor, so an age without great preaching is diseased in its vital organs. The sermon is the criteria of the vision of life in the age.

Mere sermonizing is insipid and ludicrous. The elements of art in a sermon, as we have been considering them, are but clanging cymbals if the love of man in the yearning heart is gone. Dr. Johnson said, "My dear sir, clear your mind of cant." Pulpit jargon may glitter and effervesce until the crack of doom without any good effects unless the heart is sympathetic to the human needs of the day.

There are absolutes in preaching. Our preaching will parallel the insipidity of the French Academy if we seek to make technical perfection paramount, and forget that the key to any perfection is in the ultimate idea of the mind seeking expression. Consummate expression must be balanced by communicative value in the art of the preacher. Human sympathy and understanding, a sincere attempt to find truth and express it meaningfully, and a purpose rooted in critical insight, alone make it possible for the finer elements of formal artistic perfection to reach toward the transcendent realm of meaningful expression.

NOTES

PASTORAL LANGUAGE AS BEHAVIOR: A NEW INTRODUCTION

1. Ayer, Alfred Jules, *Language, Truth and Logic* (New York: Dover, 1952), p. 34.
2. *Ibid.*, p. 35.
3. *Ibid.*, p. 37.
4. *Ibid.*, p. 44.
5. Laird, Carlton, *Miracle of Language* (Cleveland: World Publishing, 1953), p. 23.
6. Koestler, Arthur, and Smythies, J. R., eds., *Beyond Reductionism* (Boston: Beacon Press, 1969), p. 279.
7. Laird, *op. cit.*, p. 17.

CHAPTER 1, ENGAGING THE MIND

1. Dale, Edgar, *Audio-Visual Methods of Teaching* (New York: Holt, Rinehart & Winston, rev. ed. 1954).

CHAPTER 4, THE FRAMEWORK OF PREACHING

1. Altshuler, I. A., "Organism-as-a-whole and Music Therapy" in Jacob Moreno, M.D., ed., *Group Psychotherapy*

—*A Symposium* (New York: Beacon House, 1946), p. 227-228.

2. *Ibid.,* p. 229.
3. *Ibid.,* p. 229.

CHAPTER 5, GROUP RESPONSE

1. Freud, Sigmund, *Group Psychology and the Analysis of the Ego* (New York: Bantam Books, 1960), p. 16.
2. *Ibid.,* p. 17.
3. Le Bon, Gustave, *The Crowd: A Study of the Popular Mind* (New York: The Viking Company, Compass Books edition, 1960), pp. 16-17.
4. Freud, *op. cit.,* p. 32.
5. Le Bon, *op. cit.,* p. 27.
6. Le Bon, *op cit.,* p. 29.
7. Freud, *op. cit.,* p. 46.
8. Freud, *op. cit.,* p. 16.
9. McDougall, William, *The Group Mind* (New York: G. P. Putnam's Sons, 1920), p. 64.
10. Freud, Sigmund, *The Future of An Illusion* (New York: Doubleday & Co., Anchor Books, 1957), p. 102.
12. Freud, *ibid.,* p. 98.
13. Atkin, I., "Psychotherapy and the Trainee Psychotherapist," *American Journal of Psychotherapy,* January, 1950, p. 89.
14. McDougall, *op. cit.,* pp. 30-31.
15. Slavson, S. R., *Creative Group Education* (New York: Association Press, 1945), p. 16.
16. Woll, I., "Group Therapy," *American Journal of Psychotherapy,* April, 1950, p. 35.

17. Slavson, *op. cit.*, p. 86.
18. Freud, *The Future of An Illusion,* p. 30.

CHAPTER 6, GROUP DYNAMICS

1. Atkin, I., *op. cit.*, p. 88.
2. Klapman, J. W., *Group Psychotherapy, Theory and Practice* (New York: Grune and Stratton, first edition, 1946), p. 1.
3. Slavson, S. R., *An Introduction to Group Therapy* (New York: International Universities Press, 6th printing, 1954).
4. Meerloo, Joost A. M., *Patterns of Panic* (New York: International Universities Press, 2nd printing, 1952). See also *Rape of the Mind* (Cleveland: World Publishing Company) and *Two Faces of Man* (Int. Univs., 1954).
5. Adorno, T. W., *et al., The Authoritarian Personality* (New York: Harper and Brothers, 1960).

CHAPTER 7, WHERE DISCIPLINES MEET

1. Jung, Carl G., *Modern Man in Search of a Soul* (New York: Harcourt, Brace and Company, Harvest Books edition), quoted throughout this chapter.